# Sunbonnet Sue
## and Scottie Too

SUZANNE ZARUBA CIRILLO

Martingale®
& COMPANY

The author (right) and her sister, Rosemarie,
watching boats on the Erie Canal. Utica, New York, 1948.

## - DEDICATION -

*To my mother, Elizabeth Schade Zaruba,
who made all these happy childhood
memories a reality.*

*To my husband, Richard Cirillo,
whose loving support and assistance
helped this book come into being.*

*And to my beautiful family. I love you all.*

## - ACKNOWLEDGMENTS -

*I wish to thank Natalie Avery and Kittie Ellis of
Cutting Edge Quiltworks for their enthusiastic
support; Louise Mansolillo, who did the long-arm
machine quilting on all the quilts, with the exception of "Bordered in Green"; and Terry Martin of
Martingale & Company, who so generously offered
to complete "Bordered in Green."*

Sunbonnet Sue and Scottie Too
© 2007 by Suzanne Zaruba Cirillo

That Patchwork Place® is
an imprint of Martingale
& Company®.

Martingale & Company
20205 144th Ave. NE
Woodinville, WA 98072-8478
www.martingale-pub.com

**Mission Statement**
*Dedicated to
providing quality
products and
service to inspire
creativity.*

Printed in China
12 11 10 09 08 07          8 7 6 5 4 3 2 1

Library of Congress Cataloging-in-Publication Data
Library of Congress Control Number: 2006026575

ISBN: 978-1-56477-703-4

### Credits
CEO • Tom Wierzbicki
Publisher • Jane Hamada
Editorial Director • Mary V. Green
Managing Editor • Tina Cook
Technical Editor • Laurie Baker
Copy Editor • Melissa Bryan
Design Director • Stan Green
Illustrators • Laurel Strand
and Lisa McKenney
Cover and Text Designer • Regina Girard
Photographer • Brent Kane

# Contents

# Preface

Whenever I bathe my two little spaniels I usually end up completely soaked with water, which invariably necessitates a dry change of clothing. Because of this, I decided to make a puppy-bathing apron to wear whenever doing this activity. I've always enjoyed traditional-style quilts, of which Sunbonnet Sue is one, and decided to design a Sunbonnet Sue Bathing Scottie pattern to sew in redwork to decorate my apron. After designing this first pattern, the ideas began to flow one after another until I had designed an entire collection of Sues and Scotties. They were such a joy to make.

I drew the Sunbonnet Sue designs to reflect activities I did and enjoyed when I was a young girl in the late 1940s and early 1950s. I did update Sue somewhat from her traditional garb, however, to a more comfortable and practical outfit for little girls—overalls. I wore such dress as a young child and still do today. Scottie was modeled after a pet Scottish terrier named Bonnie that my mother had when she was a young woman living in Miami, Florida, in the very early 1940s.

I had such a good time drawing the patterns, and was so pleased with the results, that I wanted to share them with other quilters. After showing my patterns to a few people, they all seemed to voice the same comment: "You should get them published." So here they are, Sunbonnet Sue and Scottie, all ready to play.

# Introduction

This manuscript began as a fun collection of Sunbonnet Sue and Scottie patterns that spilled forth from my thoughts. They were designed with simplicity and authenticity in mind, and sized to finish at 9" square. They can, however, be reduced or enlarged to any size you wish. In addition to the patterns, I have presented some general thoughts and information about fabric, embroidery, redwork, appliqué, and quilt construction.

My interest in needlework goes back to when I was a small child. I have learned to do what I do by trial and error, by the kind advice of needlework enthusiasts, by watching needle-art programs on television, by taking quilt-shop classes, and by reading many excellent books and quilting magazines over the years. Learning for me is not only a joy, but a lifetime passion. Please take whatever helpful information you find here and incorporate it into your own body of knowledge. All the instructions are given from a right-hander's viewpoint. For those of you who are left-handed, please adjust the information accordingly.

The Sunbonnet Sue and Scottie patterns were created for fun. Although I designed them for making quilts, they are also perfect for wearable art, tote bags, home decor, linens, or even framed artwork to hang on the wall. So let's get started.

# *Useful Supplies to Have on Hand*

Listed in this section are some of the supplies that I used and found helpful while doing the projects presented in this book. Not all the supplies are essential to sewing the projects. Some are just "nice to have." The needlework artisans that lived so many years ago certainly didn't have all the tools that are available to us today, and their work was superb. It's fun to experiment with new methods and products, though, so you may want to give them a try.

Buy and use the best tools you can find and afford. You will put a lot of love, time, and effort into your quilting projects, and good supplies will make your work easier, the process more enjoyable, and the results better.

**All-purpose thread** for piecing your quilt top. I use Mettler 50-weight 100% cotton.

**Embroidery floss** for doing redwork, hand embroidering around appliquéd pieces, and adding detail lines. I use DMC six-strand cotton.

**Embroidery hoop** to hold your block while hand embroidering. An adjustable plastic 3" x 6" oval or 6" round will be the most useful for embroidering the blocks in this book.

**Fabrics** for your quilt top and backing. I use only 100% cotton. For more information, see "Fabric" on page 8.

**Fine-point permanent pen** to trace designs for redwork and to make quilt labels.

**Freezer paper** for stabilizing fabric when tracing embroidery designs and writing on fabric labels.

**Fusible web** to adhere fabric to fabric when doing appliqué. I use Wonder-Under.

**Glass-headed straight pins** for holding fabric pieces together. The glass head will not melt if you press over it.

**Iron-on tear-away stabilizer** to stabilize appliquéd blocks for machine stitching. I use Sulky Totally Stable.

**Light table** for tracing designs. My husband gave me one for a Christmas present. What a great gift!

**Needle-nose tweezers** work well for removing stabilizer from small machine-stitched areas.

**Needle puller** for help in grabbing the needle and pulling it through a thick area of fabric.

**Needle threader.** I keep one in my sewing box just in case it's needed.

**Needles** for hand embroidery and quilting.

**Painter's tape** for securing patterns and fabric to a light table, and for picking up loose threads on fabric pieces.

**Pencil** to trace and transfer designs. Keep it sharp.

**Plastic zippered storage bags** for keeping your blocks together and organized when you're not working on them. I generally leave the bags partially unzipped so that air can circulate through them, unless I'm using the bags to transport my blocks somewhere.

**Rotary cutter, mat, and rulers.** I use mats measuring 18" x 24" and 12" x 18". Not only do I use the mats for cutting blocks and strips, but I also like to put them under fabric to protect the table when I'm pinning. A 6" x 24" ruler is good for cutting fabric pieces, and square rulers in 12½" and 9½" sizes are good for squaring up blocks. A 1" x 6" ruler comes in handy when centering redwork or appliqué designs on the background square.

**Scissors.** I use general-purpose scissors to cut paper, and sharp fabric scissors for cutting fabric. A very fine size of embroidery scissors, such as my 3½" scissors in the shape of a stork, is nice to have for snipping threads. And I like a slightly larger size (4") for snipping threads and making small fabric cuts.

**Sewing box** to carry your embroidery items around with you.

**Sewing machine** in good working order. A simple straight-stitch machine is all you need, but one with a blanket stitch or other decorative stitch that can be used for machine appliquéing is nice.

**Spray bottle** filled with water to keep near your ironing board for spritzing stubborn wrinkles before ironing.

**Steam iron and ironing board.** I keep mine right next to my sewing machine.

**Teflon pressing sheet.** This is a great product on which to assemble appliqué pieces before adhering them to background blocks. I use one from June Tailor.

**Tracing paper** for tracing and transferring patterns.

**Transparent fluorescent tape** for rulers. Omnigrid Glow-Line Tape adheres to and removes easily from see-through rulers. Use it to highlight the desired measuring line on the ruler when you are repeatedly cutting pieces of the same size.

**White paper.** Put a sheet of white paper under the pattern when using it as a template for assembling appliqué pieces. The pattern will be easier to see.

# General Information

This section will guide you through the basics of selecting, cutting, and piecing the fabrics for your quilt. It will also cover the fundamentals of embroidery.

## - FABRIC -

I love shopping for fabric and often buy something that appeals to me, even though I don't intend to use it for my immediate project. Here are a few things to consider when buying fabrics.

### Selection

I use only 100%-cotton fabrics when making quilts. If you happen to find a polyester-and-cotton blend that is just the perfect fabric to express your thoughts, go ahead and experiment with it, but be sure to adjust the washing and ironing temperatures accordingly. Polyester will not shrink as much as cotton and cannot withstand as high an iron temperature.

When selecting fabrics for a quilt I usually try to stick with one genre, such as 1930s, folk style, or juvenile, to keep the overall feel consistent. If you find a fabric you love but it just doesn't go with the others you've selected, either smile and put it back on the shelf, or buy a piece to put in your stash for a future project.

Choose fabrics with a tight weave so they will be less likely to fray. This is especially important for appliqué pieces. When purchasing fabric, separate the layers of fabric on the bolt. Examine and feel a single layer to judge the tightness of the weave. Also look at the cut ends of the bolt to see if it is still clean or if it has begun to fray.

I generally use a solid color, such as white, ecru, or another light color, for the background of redwork or appliqué blocks. But don't entirely dismiss a darker color. I've seen embroidered redwork quilts with bright red or blue backgrounds stitched with white thread, and they were beautiful. If you want to use a print for your background, stay with a very simple subdued print or a tone-on-tone print.

Print fabrics can be used for the individual pieces of appliquéd blocks, but keep in mind the size of the finished piece and how it will look in the overall appliqué pattern.

You will need to use an ambiguous or small-scale print so that the fabric will not detract from the overall Sue and Scottie design. If you are considering a large-scale print, place a template of the appliqué piece over different areas of the print to audition the fabric first. You can always fussy cut your fabric to isolate the precise portion of the fabric design that you want to use. I was pleasantly surprised when looking for a fabric for the hot dogs in the Sue and Scottie design "Barbecuing." I found the perfect shade of reddish brown in the saddle motifs of a Southwestern print fabric in my stash.

Print fabrics also can be used for alternate blocks, sashing, or borders. Just be sure to choose a fabric that highlights your redwork or appliqué blocks and doesn't outshine them—you want the redwork or appliqué blocks to be the focal point of your finished quilt.

Be sure to keep in mind that fabrics have two sides, often with very different looks. This is especially important to remember when doing appliqué. The wrong side may have just the look you've been searching for. After choosing the lovely blue fabric for Sue's overalls in "Bordered in Blue," I wanted to find another blue for the cuffs of the overalls. The wrong side was perfect.

## Preparation

Everyone seems to have an opinion about whether fabrics should be prewashed before use. Personally, I wash and dry all my fabrics as soon as I bring them into the house so that they are ready when I want to use them. I sort fabrics by colors before washing to prevent any bleeding of one color onto another. Red dyes especially can be prone to bleeding. Each color is washed separately in hot water and detergent on a gentle cycle. This shrinks the fabric and removes sizing and any excess dyes. I dry the fabric colors separately as well, placing them in a dryer set on permanent press and leaving them in just long enough to dry. To minimize wrinkling, I remove them immediately and smooth and fold them neatly. I do not press them until I am ready to use them.

## Grain Lines

When you are ready to cut your fabrics, it is important to consider the grain lines, or the direction the threads run in the cloth. This can be important because it may affect the direction in which you want to cut and sew your quilt blocks.

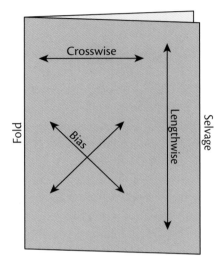

The lengthwise grain runs the length of the fabric from one cut end to the other. This grain line is the most stable and has very little, if any, stretch. I generally try to keep the lengthwise grain of the fabric pieces in line with the lengthwise direction of the quilt to minimize stretching, although this isn't always possible with directional prints and sometimes requires more fabric, especially when cutting long pieces such as borders. The finished edges along the lengthwise grain are called the selvage. The selvage is woven tighter than the rest of the fabric to keep the edge from fraying. It should always be cut off and not used for any of your quilt pieces.

Your fabric was cut off the bolt along the crosswise grain, or across the width of the fabric. This grain line has more stretch than the lengthwise grain. Hold a piece of your fabric crosswise and give it a gentle tug. You can generally tell which direction your quilt blocks are just by giving them a gentle tug.

Bias is the line diagonal to the lengthwise and crosswise grains. It has the greatest amount of stretch. Be sure to handle anything cut on the bias, including appliqué pieces, very carefully to avoid stretching the pieces out of shape. Never use steam on raw, bias-cut edges, because they can warp easily.

# – ROTARY CUTTING –

Cutting quilt blocks with a rotary cutter is a fast and efficient method. By combining rotary cutting with chain piecing, you can assemble quilt blocks in a very short time. All the quilt pieces for the projects in this book can be rotary cut, with the exception of the appliqué shapes. These will need to be cut out using scissors.

**1** Before cutting any strips with the rotary cutter, you will need to first straighten your fabric piece. Fold the fabric piece in half lengthwise, aligning the selvages. Lay the folded fabric piece on the cutting mat, positioning the cut end of the fabric to your right. If the fabric piece is long, part of it may extend off the mat to the left. Gently smooth the fabric so the folded edge lies smooth without any ripples, being sure to keep the selvages lying evenly on top of each other. If the fabric piece has warped during washing, the cut ends may not lie as evenly as when they were first cut from the bolt. That is OK. The important thing now is that when the fabric is folded in half lengthwise, selvage to selvage, the center fold of the fabric lies smooth and flat without any ripples.

**2** Place your ruler across the fabric piece close to the end lying on the mat, being sure that the ruler does not stick out over the cut ends. Line up a horizontal line on the ruler with the fabric fold. Line up another horizontal line on the ruler with the fabric selvage edge. Whenever possible, you should use at least two points of reference when using the see-through ruler and rotary cutter. With the rotary cutter, trim off the ragged end of the fabric and discard.

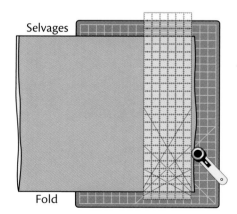

Selvages

Fold

**3** After straightening the fabric piece, loosely accordion fold the unstraightened end of the fabric piece up onto the cutting mat. Carefully turn the mat 180° so that it now faces opposite its original direction. You are now ready to cut strips from the fabric. Cut the strips in the same manner that you straightened the fabric, always using at least two points of reference on the ruler to position the ruler on the fabric. You can use the folded center edge of the fabric, the straightened cut edge, and the selvage edge as reference points. Sometimes the large fabric piece shifts somewhat while you are cutting strips, and you will need to straighten it up again. Do this by the same method used previously.

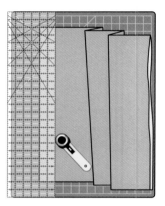

**4** After cutting the long strips across the width of the fabric piece, you can cut the strips into squares and rectangles. Do this using the same method you used when cutting strips from the fabric piece, being sure to remove the selvage from the end of the strip first, and cutting through one layer of fabric at a time. Line up your see-through ruler on the strip, using the top and bottom of the strip as reference points, and crosscut (cut across the strip's width) to the size specified in the quilt instructions.

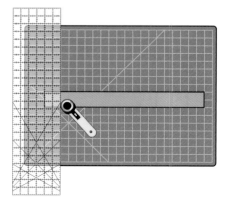

A rotary cutter is extremely sharp. Think of it as a circular razor blade. Be very careful when using it. Here are some rules that I follow while cutting with the rotary cutter.

- Never cut with the rotary cutter when you are tired. You need to be totally alert when using this blade. If you're tired, do something else.

- Do not use the rotary cutter if children or pets may distract you. You need to keep your total attention on your cutting.

- Always wear shoes when cutting with the rotary cutter. On the remote chance you drop the cutter, your feet will have some protection.

- Stand up while cutting. You'll have more control.

- Always cut away from yourself. Be aware of where your hands, fingers, and arms are while you are cutting.

- Cut slowly.

- Always, without fail, close the safety on the rotary cutter after each and every cut—no exceptions. Close the safety immediately upon completion of the cut before lifting the rotary cutter up off the mat.

- Have a designated place where you set down the rotary cutter between cuts. Put it in this place every time.

- Have a designated safe place where you store the rotary cutter when not in use, preferably in a closed container of some sort. Put it in this place each and every time you are done using it.

## - CHAIN PIECING -

Chain piecing is a quick and efficient method of sewing your quilt pieces together in an assembly-line manner. You can use this technique when assembling blocks, joining blocks, sewing sashing to blocks, or joining rows of blocks.

❶ Place the first two pieces that are to be sewn together under the presser foot, right sides together. Sew the seam, stopping at the end with the needle in the fabric. Do not remove the pieces.

❷ Feed the next pair of pieces to be sewn together under the presser foot. Continue feeding the units to be sewn through the machine without cutting between them. You should now have a long chain of stitched pairs.

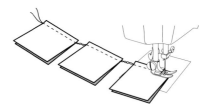

❸ When all the units have been sewn, remove the chain from the machine, cutting the thread close to the last unit sewn. If the order in which the pieces were sewn is not important, cut the thread tail at the beginning of the chain and the connecting stitching between the blocks. Stack the paired pieces on your ironing board for pressing or set them aside.

If the sewing order of the units is important, carry the chain to your design area and lay the pieces down in their proper positions, using the thread tail as an indicator as to which block was sewn first. After you are satisfied that the blocks are all in their proper places, cut the connecting threads, including the thread tail.

## - PRESSING -

When making a quilt, your iron and ironing board are as important to you as your sewing machine. Don't be tempted to bypass the important step of pressing. You have, of course, already ironed your fabrics before cutting any pieces; but you will also need to press the seam allowances of the pieced blocks after you've joined them, being careful to press every seam allowance before crossing it with another seam. On rare occasions I finger-press, or use my thumbnail to press, a short seam allowance to one side before crossing it with another seam, but generally I press seam allowances using a hot iron so that they lie flat and smooth.

There is some difference of opinion among quilters as to whether seam allowances should be pressed open or to one side. I press seam allowances to one side. Usually I press toward the darker fabric, but not always. Sometimes when sewing rows of pieced blocks together to assemble a quilt top, I press the first row of seam allowances all to the right, the second row of seam allowances all to the left, the third row to the right, and so forth. Pressing in this manner causes the rows of seam allowances to interlock as they are sewn together. In this particular instance the seam allowances are not all necessarily being pressed toward the darker fabric.

You can, however, press all the seam allowances toward the darker fabric if you prefer, and in some cases it's a better method. If you press in this manner, you will need to be more careful to watch how the seam allowances lie as you come to them when stitching. You may want to pin them beforehand so that they won't fold over and be sewn in the wrong direction as you stitch over them. If this occurs, the seam allowances might not interlock properly.

Until seam allowances are really sewn down securely, I press by using an up-and-down motion to bring the iron into contact with the fabric. At this point I don't actually iron in the sense of sliding the iron across the fabric, because that could easily cause the fabric to warp. Using a dry iron also helps prevent fabric distortion.

I use the following method when pressing seam allowances to one side. Pressing in this manner will help prevent unwanted pleating in the seam lines and help your quilts lie smoother.

❶ Lay the stitched-together fabric on your ironing board just as it was sewn, keeping the two right sides of the fabric together, one on top of the other. The wrong side of the fabric toward which you want the seam allowance pressed should be face up on the ironing board.

❷ Leaving the fabrics layered, gently press the stitching you just sewed by lifting your iron straight up and down over the stitching.

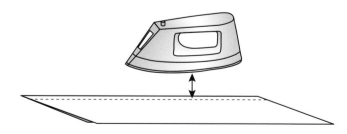

❸ Gently slide the iron between the two layers of fabric you just pressed. Lift the top layer of fabric up and over the newly sewn seam as you press along the seam line. As you press, the fabrics should lie in their

proper position next to each other, with the seam allowance between them pressed neatly to one side.

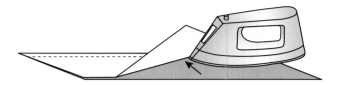

When you are pressing pieced units or blocks, you can chain press them just as you chain pieced. Stack the blocks on one end of the ironing board. Pick them up one at a time and press as described previously, restacking them on another spot of the ironing board. If the pieced blocks are chained together with connecting threads, you don't need to cut the connecting threads before pressing. Just lay part of the string of blocks on the ironing board, press, and continue working down the chain. After pressing, arrange the blocks on your design area in their proper places. If the blocks do not need to be in any particular order yet, cut the connecting threads and stack the blocks.

After your quilt top is completed, you will want to give it a good press. If necessary, use some steam or a little spray from your bottle of water. You also can dip your finger in water and dab the area that needs a little extra help. That way you're not dampening the entire quilt top.

## - EMBROIDERY -

Hand embroidery is peaceful and relaxing to me. It can be done anywhere, whether I'm sitting under the big mulberry tree in my backyard or riding to Tucson in the car with my husband to visit our daughter. I just put my supplies in a small sewing box and I'm ready to go. Here are a few things to keep in mind when doing embroidery.

### *Threading the Needle*

I used one strand of DMC six-strand embroidery floss to stitch all the redwork blocks and the embroidery handwork in the appliqué blocks shown in this book. If you desire a heavier line, stitch the patterns with more than one strand.

To separate one strand of floss from the six-strand skein, first cut a piece, roughly 14" to 18" long, from the skein. Pieces longer than 18" tend to tangle, wear thin, fray, and break as you stitch. Hold one end of the floss lightly between your left thumb and forefinger, leaving a short length of the floss extending above your fingers and letting the rest of the length hang straight down. With your right hand, lightly run your thumb and forefinger down the piece of floss to eliminate any kinks or curls. Still using your right hand, gently separate one strand of floss from the end of the floss that is extending above your left thumb and forefinger. Slowly and gently pull this strand straight up. After separating the single strand, smooth out the remaining cut piece. If you want to sew with more than one strand, remove the strands from the length of floss one at a time, smoothing out the floss after each strand is removed, and then rejoin the separated strands.

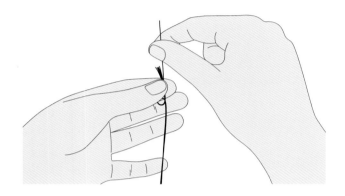

You are now ready to thread your needle. I use either quilting needles or embroidery needles to embroider. The quilting needle is shorter and has a smaller eye than the embroidery needle, and seems to give me good control over the stitches. The embroidery needle has a longer eye, is easier to thread, and will better accommodate more strands of floss than the quilting needle. Use whichever needle is more comfortable for you. Choose a needle that doesn't have too large of an eye, however, because it may leave visible holes in your fabric.

There is some difference of opinion about whether to knot the end of the thread when doing embroidery so that it doesn't pull out of the fabric. Some folks prefer to interweave the thread ends through the stitching on the back of the embroidery piece rather than knot the thread. I personally feel a little uncomfortable with this and knot all my threads, both when I start sewing with a thread and when I finish sewing.

## Using an Embroidery Hoop

I use an adjustable 4" x 6" oval or 6" round hoop when embroidering. The hoop keeps the fabric taut so the stitches are even and lie properly, without puckering the fabric or being too tight or too loose. An adjustable hoop consists of two oval-shaped or circular hoops—a larger outer hoop with a thumbscrew, and a smaller inner hoop.

To put a fabric piece into a hoop, first loosen the thumbscrew to open up the outer hoop. Lay the fabric piece over the inner hoop, positioning the area where you want to sew in the center of the hoop. Carefully place the outer hoop over the fabric and inner hoop, and then tighten the thumbscrew to hold the fabric taut. I generally place the thumbscrew in an upper-left position if possible, because the floss is less likely to catch on it as I stitch.

To remove the hoop from the fabric, first loosen the thumbscrew to open up the outer hoop. Lift the outer hoop off the fabric piece slowly, just in case the hoop has caught on some threads. I always open the hoop to one side, choosing the side of the hoop that has no stitching underneath it. After the first side of the hoop is lifted, lift the rest of the hoop upward. Opening the hoop in this manner should help prevent any damage to your work.

## *The Stitches*

I used the following embroidery stitches when stitching the Sue and Scottie designs.

**Stem stitch.** The stem stitch is used for most of the Sue and Scottie designs done in redwork as well as for most of the detail lines on the appliqué blocks. The solid lines on the designs indicate when to use the stem stitch. Use short stitches, especially along tight curves. Keep the excess thread coming out of your needle on the same side of the stitched line as the outside curve of the traced line. If the traced line changes direction, change the side where the excess thread lies, using a small stitch or two when changing the direction of your thread. If you are sewing a sharp point in the traced line, tack down the stitch at that point as you sew.

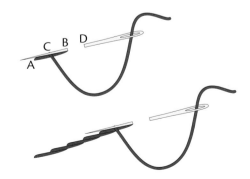

**Running stitch.** Use a running stitch wherever a short dashed line is shown on the designs. Be sure to keep the stitches the same tautness as your fabric—not too tight or too loose. Sometimes I insert the needle straight up and down perpendicular to the fabric when sewing the running stitch, taking one stitch at a time.

**Cross-stitch.** Cross-stitches are used for the laces of Sue's shoes and are indicated by Xs on the designs. Keep each X crossed in the same direction for a neater look.

**French knot.** French knots are shown as a single dot on the designs. Wrap the thread around the needle two or more times, depending on how large you want the knot to be. Insert the needle back through the fabric next to where it originally came out. Hold the knot in place with your left hand while gently pulling the needle to the wrong side of the fabric with your right.

**Satin stitch.** Satin stitches are used for the rounded tips of the jacks in "Playing Jacks" and are shown on the pattern as circles with lines running through them. Position your stitches close together. I made three to four stitches at each tip.

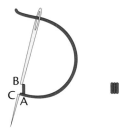

**Blanket stitch.** The blanket stitch can be used to secure appliqué shapes in place after they have been fused to the background. Be aware of the curvature of the appliqué shape as you stitch. The line of stitching on the outside edge of the appliqué should outline the shape, with the fingers of the stitching inward and perpendicular to the edge.

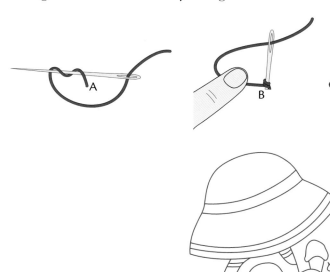

# Making the Blocks

You have two alternatives for creating the block designs: redwork or appliqué. Both techniques begin with a background square cut at least 1" larger on each side than the desired finished size of the square. Cutting the square larger allows for any reduction caused by the embroidery or appliqué, and allows more room for the embroidery hoop to attach to the fabric. The extra fabric will be cut away after the completed block is squared up to its proper measurement. The extra allowance is reflected in the cutting instructions for the individual projects.

## – REDWORK –

Redwork, like other embroidery, can easily be carried with you anywhere you go. Once you've traced and drawn the design, you can stitch the square at your convenience, anywhere, anytime.

### Tracing the Design

Be sure your hands are clean before starting.

❶ Trace the chosen design onto tracing paper using a dark-colored permanent marking pen. If you wish to make any changes to the design, do so now on the paper tracing. Let the ink dry completely.

❷ Find a good light source where you can trace the pattern onto the background square. A sunny window works well. A light table, if you have one, works even better because you can lay your work down flat. With a small piece of painter's tape or masking tape, tape down each corner of the traced pattern over the light source so that it doesn't move. If you want to reverse the design from its original direction, simply turn over the traced pattern.

❸ Place the background square on the ironing board, right side down. Press thoroughly, keeping track of the grain lines if you wish. (If you want to keep the lengthwise grain of the quilt blocks in line with the lengthwise direction of the quilt, give the square a little tug in both directions to determine the crosswise and lengthwise grain lines.)

❹ Cut a square of freezer paper slightly smaller than the background square. Place it shiny side down on the wrong side of the background square, and press it into place with a hot iron. The freezer paper will adhere to the fabric and stabilize it while you trace the design onto the square. After tracing the design, you can remove the freezer paper easily. You may use this same piece of freezer paper over and over again. If you decide not to use freezer paper to stabilize the square, you can still trace the design, but you will need to be more careful that the fabric doesn't ripple as you trace. Rippling can cause the traced lines to not meet up properly, resulting in a crooked design.

❺ Place the square, freezer paper down, over the taped-down pattern on your light source, aligning the lengthwise fabric grain line vertically if desired. Use a small see-through ruler to help center the block over the design, measuring from a major element of the pattern to each side of the square. Stand back and look at the pattern placement on the square. If it looks a little off center, center it by sight.

6 Tape each corner of the fabric square over the design, securing two diagonal corners first, and then taping the remaining two corners.

7 Get comfortable before tracing onto the fabric. I often put two pillows on the seat of my chair to raise myself to a comfortable height while using my light table. I also play the radio. Do whatever helps you stay relaxed. If you make a few wavy lines as you trace, don't worry—you can just sew up the center of the wave as you embroider.

If you are using a light table, be sure that the table sits securely on all four feet or it may suddenly tip over while you are tracing. This has happened to me on more than one occasion when tracing. Pick the light table up and turn it around instead of reaching across it to trace the pattern. This will keep your hands more relaxed and help prevent smears on the block. I struggled across my light table for some time before it occurred to me that I could simply move the table around instead of reaching across it.

8 Trace the design slowly and lightly onto your background square, using a fabric marking pencil or fine-line permanent pen. If you use a permanent pen, use the color that you intend to stitch with if possible. Be sure to always check the pen you intend to use for permanence, regardless of the assurances on the label. I've had to resew blocks because a "permanent" pen's color ran when the ink got wet. Ask at your quilt store to see if the pen you intend to use needs to have its color set, and find out what the procedure is for doing so.

Be sure to close the pen when you set it down. This helps prevent it from drying out or forming globs of ink on its tip. Blot the tip of your pen frequently when tracing so that you won't get blotches of ink along the tracing lines, especially when starting or stopping a line. If possible, start and end a line of tracing at an intersection in the lines of the design. This helps keep little globs of ink from collecting along a long straight stitching line in the pattern. Be sure to keep hands

away from any work already traced. You don't want to smear it.

If you cannot see the design clearly under the square while tracing the pattern, lift up the corner of the square and peek under. Secure the fabric again at the corner after checking the pattern.

9 After completing the tracing, check to see that you reproduced the complete design. Lift up a corner of the square to check the design underneath, comparing it to the traced design on the block. Try not to disturb the taped-down pattern or the background square in case you forgot something. After you are satisfied that the complete pattern has been transferred, remove the tape from the fabric and pattern. Gently remove the freezer paper from the wrong side of the fabric and set it aside to use on the next block.

### Stitching the Design

All the redwork shown in this book was stitched with one strand of DMC six-strand embroidery floss, color 498. I was told that this shade is similar to the red color used in traditional redwork quilts. You may, of course, use any number of strands or colors of floss that you choose, depending on the effect you wish to achieve. Using a single strand allows you to stitch three or four of the patterns on pages 44–79 with one skein of embroidery floss.

Before you begin stitching, position yourself and your light source so that you have an adequate amount of light in your work area. Make sure your stitching hand does not cast a shadow over your work. Check the color identification number of your floss, especially when starting a new skein, so that your redwork color remains consistent.

Decide where you want to begin stitching. Think of the design lines as a type of maze. You want to avoid as many knots as you can. You also want, as much as possible, to avoid carrying the thread across the wrong side of the design from one area to another; the knots and carry-over threads may shadow through the background fabric. Except for "On a Trapeze," "On Stilts," "Planting Flowers," and "Swinging," I started each design by stitching Sue's hat, beginning where the lower-left side of her hatband intersects with the hat. In the four designs previously mentioned, another part of the design crosses over the hat. In these four designs I started stitching by first working the elements that cross over the hat. After sewing these cross-over elements, I sewed the hat. By sewing the hat first—or, in the case of the four pattern exceptions, their cross-over elements and then the hats—you can use the stitching on the wrong side of the hat through which to weave your thread as you move on to sew Sue's shirt and overalls.

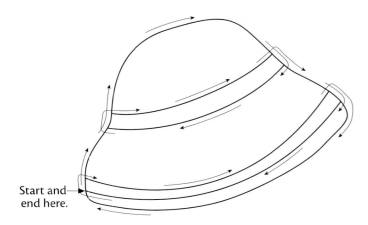

Start and end here.

Begin stitching the back of Sue's shirt at the intersection of the lower part of the shirt and Sue's back. Work up the shirt toward the hat, and weave the floss through the stitching on the wrong side of the block on the hat's brim to the intersection of Sue's hat and her neck or back. Next, start stitching down Sue's back. At the lower part of the pocket, turn into the pocket and sew around the entire pocket, ending up at the top of the pocket again. Weave the floss in the stitching underneath Sue's back until it comes to where it left off, and then continue stitching down her back. Always be sure to weave the thread through the stitching on the wrong side, keeping the floss underneath the stitching line and coming up next to the next element of the design. You can use this technique anywhere in the design, but you need to plan ahead.

*Hat*

Weave through backside.

*Shirt*

*Overalls*

Start here.

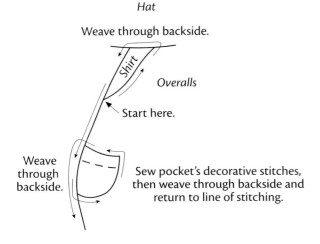

Weave through backside.

Sew pocket's decorative stitches, then weave through backside and return to line of stitching.

To begin stitching, gently drag the tip of the needle along the wrong side of the background square so that you can see a small rise on the front of the block. Stop dragging the needle when the rise reaches the point where you want to begin stitching. Insert your needle into the fabric and pull the needle up until the knot stops it. Stitch on the traced lines, using the stitches indicated on the pattern. Refer to "The Stitches" on page 13 for specifics on making each stitch.

I make it a rule not to carry thread more than ¼" from any one element of the design to another across the wrong side of the fabric. When sewing bubbles, as in "Bathing Scottie" and "Blowing Bubbles," start stitching on a line where two bubbles are closest to each other so that you can first stitch around one bubble and then carry your thread the shortest distance to the next bubble. When stitching Sue's shoes, work across from the closest stem-stitched line, do the cross-stitches, and then work your way back to where you left off the stem-stitched line. Do the same when stitching Scottie's eyes.

If your floss becomes worn or frizzy while stitching, knot it off on the wrong side of the block to prevent breakage while you are stitching. When knotting the floss, knot slowly, being careful not to catch the thread of the loop with the needle, or it could easily knot up prematurely.

When beginning with a new piece of floss, use your forefinger under the hoop to hold the knot out of the way of the needle when sewing the first stitch. Otherwise the needle may catch the knot and tangle up the thread underneath the hoop.

Whenever I stop sewing, in addition to loosening the hoop, I put my needle to rest either in a traced line that is not yet sewn, or in the very edge of the background square in a seam allowance. That way I won't put unnecessary holes in the fabric with my needle.

### Completing the Block

After completing the redwork, remove the embroidered square from the hoop and check to see that all the traced lines have been stitched. Carefully press the block by laying it right side down over a pressing cloth, covering it with another pressing cloth. I use clean, white men's handkerchiefs for pressing cloths. Square up (trim to a square shape) the block to the size called for in the project instructions, keeping the design centered.

# – APPLIQUÉ –

Of the different methods of sewing appliqué, I chose to use the fusing method. It's durable and has a casual look that I like.

### Tracing the Design

Before tracing the separate appliqué pieces of the design, you need to first trace the complete design onto tracing paper. You will use this tracing-paper drawing not only to help you to trace the individual parts of the patterns, but also to help you in assembling the pieces into the final design. Follow the same process used for tracing a design done in redwork. (See "Tracing the Design" on page 15.)

When designing the patterns, I gave Sue a variety of shirtsleeve styles. In appliqué, you may wish to use the simplest shirtsleeves, and you may also wish to omit the shirt necklines in those designs that have them. In many of the designs, Sue's overalls have pant cuffs. If you wish to further simplify the patterns, leave out the cuffs and trace the pant legs a little longer to compensate. Remember that you do not need to appliqué all the elements in the design. Feel free to embroider some of the accessory parts of the designs.

### Creating the Appliqué Shapes

After tracing the entire design onto tracing paper, you will need to use the tracing-paper pattern to transfer the separate elements of the design to the paper side of the fusible web to create the appliqué shapes. Before you can do this, you need to decide in which order the pieces will be assembled to create the design. Decide which elements go on top of, or underneath, other elements of the design. Elements that are under another element will need to have an extension added to them. For example, Sue's arm is positioned under her sleeve. You will need to add a short extension to the top of her arm as you trace it onto the fusible web. Draw this extension as you trace Sue's arm. The extension will later be positioned and fused underneath

the sleeve. The same is true of Sue's shoes, which will be positioned underneath the pant legs of her overalls.

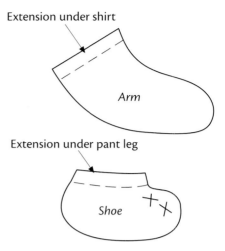

If you are including cuffs on Sue's overalls, the cuffs will always be positioned over the bottom of her pant legs and top of her shoes. You will need to add a small extension to both the bottom of her pant legs and the top of her shoes. After layering the pant legs, shoes, and cuffs in their proper positions, the cuffs will lie on top of both pant legs and shoes.

Trace the front and back of Sue's shirt as one unit. Draw an extension around most of the piece, except for the edges that will not be overlapped by another piece.

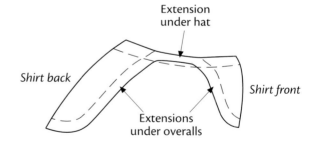

In most patterns, Sue's hat will be the last shape added. The hat goes on top of everything else and has nothing overlapping it. You will be able to trace the hat exactly as it is shown on the pattern and will not need to add an extension.

When you are ready to trace the individual design elements on the transfer web, place the tracing-paper drawing on the light box with the blank side up and the traced side facing down on the light box. This is important if you want the completed design to face the same direction as in the original pattern. If you want Sue and Scottie to appear in reverse of the original pattern, place the tracing-paper image right side up on the light box.

When tracing onto the web, use a pencil or pen to transfer the design lines onto the paper side of the fusible web. Draw the cutting line of the element with a solid line and use a dotted line where an element meets up with, and goes under, another element. Leave a little space around each element when you are tracing. This will give you some cutting room all around the piece.

Always label every element as you trace it. A shoe may look like a shoe when you draw it, but later on, it might be difficult to recognize. Write your label right side up on the tracing so that you can tell which part of the element is the top or bottom. Be sure to label the shoes and arms as F (front) and B (back) when appropriate. Trace any additional design lines of the element, such as leg separations, overalls stitching lines, and so on. You will need these lines later when you are embroidering the details.

After tracing all the elements onto the fusible web, cut around each of the individual pieces, but do not cut on the drawn lines yet.

Now is the time to pull out all those wonderful scraps you've been saving. Sometimes even the smallest scrap is just the perfect piece of fabric you're looking for. Choose the fabrics that you wish to use for Sue, Scottie, and any other appliquéd elements. Press them if needed.

Place a piece of the chosen fabric wrong side up on your ironing board. Position the appropriate fusible-web shape over it, paper side up. You may want to keep in mind the fabric grain lines during this step so that the grain lines of the shape match up with the grain lines of the fabric. If you want to cut out a particular design of the fabric pattern, or want the fabric pattern to lie at a particular angle, ignore the grain lines. When everything is lined up as you want, follow the manufacturer's instructions to fuse the shape to the fabric. Keep in mind that pencil or pen marks sometimes smear when ironed over. Be careful that they do not smear onto your fabric or iron soleplate. Press carefully.

After the fabric and fusible web have cooled, cut out the shape. I find that it is easier to first cut away the fused fabric from the large fabric piece, and then cut out the shape on the marked lines. I usually hold the scissors in one position, turning the fabric piece as I work.

## Assembling the Design

After all the appliqué shapes are cut out, you can assemble the design. I find that the easiest way to do this is to use a Teflon pressing sheet to adhere all the elements of the Sue appliqué together as one unit before fusing it onto the background fabric.

Place a blank sheet of white paper on your ironing board. This will help your tracing-paper pattern show up better. Place the traced pattern over the blank paper, right side up. On top of the pattern, place the Teflon pressing sheet. You are now ready to begin fusing.

Remove the paper backing from the appliqué shapes one at a time as you are ready to fuse each element. Carefully insert a fingernail between the paper backing and the webbing to separate them from each other, and slowly pull off the paper. I like to start separating the paper from the backing in an area of the element that goes underneath something else if possible, just in case the fabric frays a little as it is being separated from the paper. If it is difficult to start the separation, try folding the element in half to create a crease, and then start at the crease. You can also use a straight pin to score the paper to start the separation, being careful not to mark the fabric piece itself. Save any paper backings that have detail markings on them to use as a reference when stitching.

Assemble the smaller units of the design first, being careful not to rush while positioning the elements. They can slip and slide around very easily. Begin by placing Sue's hat on the pressing sheet over the proper place on the tracing-paper pattern. Give it a slight touch with a dry iron to stick it to the sheet. Place the hatband over the hat in its proper position, and touch the iron to the juncture of the hat and hatband so they will lightly fuse together. You may also assemble Sue's arm and sleeve using this same method. Because the elements are only lightly fused together, you can still take them apart easily if you need to without damaging the fabric.

Let these elements cool, and then carefully lift them from the pressing sheet. Check the junctures of the hat and hatband, and the sleeve and arm, to make sure they match up properly. If you need to trim an ever-so-little amount, do so now. Set these units aside.

Now begin to fuse Sue together. Place the overalls on the pressing sheet in the proper position. Tap them with your iron to stick them into place. Tuck Sue's shirt underneath the overalls, lightly fusing it into place. If you need to trim for a smooth transition between the overalls and shirt, let the elements cool, remove them from the pressing sheet, and carefully do so. Replace the overalls on the pressing sheet, tap with your dry iron to stick them in place, and continue layering the elements in order, using your tracing-paper pattern as a guide.

If an element of the design goes both on top of and below another element, you may need to cut a small slit in the fabric along the design line. In "Getting a Drink," you will need to cut a small slit along the design line indicating the bottom of Scottie's front leg. This will allow you to position Sue's arm both on top of Scottie's body as she holds him, and also below Scottie as her hand goes underneath his front leg.

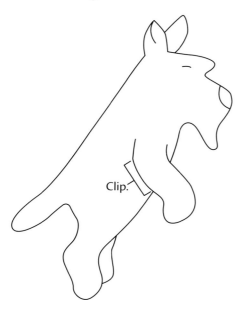

In "On Stilts," you will need to cut a small slit on the design line indicating the top of Sue's hand. You will then be able to position the stilts both on top of Sue's upper arm and underneath her hand.

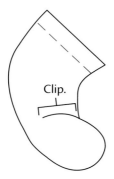

If you have difficulty seeing the tracing-paper pattern through the pressing sheet while assembling the elements, carry the pattern, pressing sheet, and appliqué pieces to your light table or other light source and assemble them there, returning to the ironing board to lightly fuse them into place. You may also use the paper backings that you saved from the fusible web to help you assemble the pieces while they are still on the ironing board. After Sue is totally assembled and lightly fused, carefully remove her from the pressing sheet.

To position the design onto the background square, first check the fabric grain lines of the square to be sure they are running in the desired directions. Center the square over the tracing-paper drawing, right side up. Use a ruler to check both sides and the top and bottom to make sure the square is completely centered. After the square is centered, position the design elements on the block using the tracing-paper pattern as a placement guide and lightly fuse in place. Remove the square from the pressing sheet and then permanently fuse the design in place following the manufacturer's instructions.

### Stitching the Design

After the appliqué shapes are fused in place, you can sew around the elements by hand or machine, using a blanket stitch or other decorative stitch. Be sure to sew over all raw edges of the fabric. (Refer to "The Stitches" on page 13 for specifics for making the hand-stitched blanket stitch.) I personally enjoy doing handwork, and often sew around the appliqué shapes with embroidery floss. Use as many strands as you need to achieve the look you want. Choose a floss color that matches your appliqué or, for a vintage look, use all black. If you cannot find a floss color that exactly matches your fabric, choose one that is slightly darker than the fabric so it will blend nicely.

If you stitch your appliqués by machine, refer to your owner's manual to set up your machine properly. Use an iron-on stabilizer on the back of your background squares, if necessary, to keep your stitches neat and your fabric from rippling.

Use 100%-cotton thread to machine sew your decorative stitches. The natural fibers of the thread will lie up against each other better than a polyester thread. I use the same color thread in both the bobbin and on the top of the machine. I know it is a big temptation not to change the bobbin with each color, but I'd rather not take the chance of a different color bobbin thread showing through to the front of the square. Sew all the elements, in all the squares, that require the same thread color before changing your thread.

Sew slowly, turning the square when necessary. If you have a needle-down function on your sewing machine, turn it on. If your sewing machine starts going too fast while sewing, stop and start slowly again. Watch the needle as you sew. It's easier to keep the outside edge of the decorative stitches at the very edges of the appliqué that way. Practice sewing your stitches on a fabric scrap first. Use an iron-on stabilizer underneath your scrap, if you plan to do so when you sew your squares.

Leave a tail of thread at the beginning and end of each sewing line, being careful not to sew over the tails as you stitch. Check often to make sure that you do not catch the bobbin tails underneath the square as you sew. After completing the square, thread the tails on the right side of the square one at a time into a needle and stitch them to the back of the square. Tie off the tails from the right side of the square to the bobbin tails in a double knot; trim them off.

### *Completing the Block*

After completing the stitching around the appliqués, remove any iron-on stabilizer from the wrong side of the block, using tweezers to remove the stabilizer from small areas. Trace and hand embroider any design detail lines. Check for and remove any loose threads. Press the block. Square up the block to the size called for in the project instructions, keeping the design centered.

# Putting It All Together

Once your blocks are stitched or appliquéd, you can complete your quilt. This section will guide you through the process of sewing your blocks together and finishing your quilt.

## ASSEMBLING
### - THE QUILT TOP -

Before sewing the quilt top together, lay out all the blocks and sashing strips on a flat surface or design wall according to the quilt instructions. You can easily make a design wall by pinning a flat, white flannel sheet up on the wall with straight pins. Smooth the blocks as you put them up on the flannel. If needed, rearrange the Sue and Scottie blocks to create a balanced layout. Sometimes I take a digital picture of the layout after I'm satisfied with the arrangement, and print it out on a piece of inexpensive paper. I can then refer to this printout as I work. Digital printouts are a good way to compare different arrangements too.

To keep the quilt top straight and squared when sewing, I use the following chain-piecing method. Refer to "Chain Piecing" on page 11 for more information.

### Quilts without Sashing

❶ Working from left to right, chain piece the first and second blocks in each row together. Remove the chain from your sewing machine and lay it back down on the design area so that the blocks are in their proper positions. Cut the connecting threads between each of the rows.

❷ Repeat step 1 to chain piece the remaining blocks in each row into pairs. Place each chain of paired blocks back in position on your design area before sewing the next pair. If you have an odd number of blocks in the row, chain piece the last block to the pair next to it.

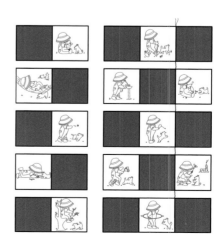

**③** Chain piece the first two pairs of blocks in each row together. Remove the chain from your sewing machine and lay it back down on the design area so that the blocks are in their proper positions. Cut the connecting threads between each of the rows. Continue in this manner until all the pairs have been sewn together to complete the rows. If you are working with an odd number of blocks, add the three-block units to the ends of the rows.

**④** Press the seam allowances in opposite directions from row to row, or if you prefer, press toward the darker fabric. Lay the pressed strips of blocks on the design area in their proper positions.

**⑤** Sew the rows together in pairs first, and then sew the pairs together. If you are working with an odd number of rows, sew the last row to the last pair. The seam allowances in each row should oppose each other. Press the seam allowances connecting the rows toward the bottom of the quilt. Give your completed top a final press, being careful not to catch any threads when pressing embroidered blocks.

### Quilts with Sashing

Quilts with sashing are sewn together in the same manner as those without. Treat your sashing strips like blocks, joining blocks and sashing strips into pairs. Treat a sashing strip between rows as a row of blocks.

## – ADDING BORDERS –

If your borders are longer than the width of your border fabric, you will need to piece them. The seam lines of the strip can be placed either centered or off center along the edge of your quilt. Placing them off center uses less fabric. I chose to center my border seam lines, and all construction information in this manuscript reflects that method.

**①** Measuring tools can be slightly different lengths. Always use the same tool for measuring your quilt top as you do for your border strips. Measure the quilt length in several places, along seam lines or other stable areas. If the measurements are different, determine the average. Trim two border strips to this measurement. If your border strips have been pieced, keep the seam line centered. Trim the excess from each end.

**②** Pin the borders to the sides of the quilt, matching centers and ends. Sew into place, easing the fabric as necessary. Press the seam allowances toward the borders. Square up the corners if necessary.

**③** Measure the quilt width—including the side borders—in several places. Trim two border strips to this measurement, keeping the seam line centered. Pin and sew the borders to the top and bottom edges of the quilt in the same manner as the side borders. Press the seam allowances toward the borders. Then square up the corners if necessary.

**④** Add any remaining borders in the same manner.

## PREPARING THE
## - BACKING AND BATTING -

Choose a backing fabric that is the same weight as the fabrics used in the quilt top. Your backing should be at least 4" longer and wider than your quilt top. Piece your backing fabric together if necessary to make a large enough piece. I use a ½"-wide seam allowance when piecing a backing to give it more stability. Long-arm machine quilters often have different size requirements for the backing, so be sure to check with your quilter if you plan to use this service.

Purchase a batting that will give you the look and feel you desire for your finished quilt. After you bring the batting home, spread it out and let it relax for at least 24 hours. Cut your batting approximately the same size as your backing.

## ASSEMBLING AND
## - FASTENING THE LAYERS -

If you plan on quilting your quilt yourself, you will need to make a "quilt sandwich" (a term used to describe the layers of a quilt prepared for basting—the backing, batting, and quilt top, layered together in that order). If you are sending your quilt to a long-arm machine quilter, check with her for specific instructions before purchasing batting or assembling the layers.

❶ Place the backing, wrong side up, on a large, flat surface. Smooth out any wrinkles. Fasten each corner to the surface with painter's tape. Check to make sure you have not created any waves in the backing while taping. Put additional small pieces of tape along the edges of the backing so that it is held securely in place.

❷ Center the batting over the backing. Gently pat out any wrinkles, starting at the center and working outward.

❸ Carefully remove any loose threads on both the front and back of the quilt top. Trim any threads that are still attached. Fold the quilt top into quarters, right sides together. Place it over the batting so that it will be centered and in the proper position when unfolded. Gently unfold the quilt, making sure that it is right side up. The batting and backing should extend beyond the quilt top on all sides.

❹ Baste the layers together with thread or safety pins. With either method, begin basting at the center of the quilt and work out toward the edges, basting in a grid pattern of lines roughly 4" apart. After completing the basting, remove the painter's tape from the backing fabric.

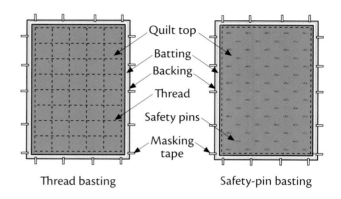

Quilt top
Batting
Backing
Thread
Safety pins
Masking tape

Thread basting                    Safety-pin basting

❺ Hand or machine quilt, or tie the layers together.

❻ Square up the quilt, being careful not to cut into any quilting lines or ties that might undo your hard work.

## - MAKING A HANGING SLEEVE -

If you plan to display your finished quilt on a wall, consider sewing a hanging sleeve to the back of the quilt. This should be done before binding the quilt edges. I like to make my hanging sleeves with fabric that matches the backing material, so I always purchase a little extra for this purpose.

❶ Measure the width of the quilt as you would for borders (see "Adding Borders" on page 23). Cut a strip of fabric 8½" x the width of your quilt, piecing the strip if necessary.

❷ Press the ends under ¼" and stitch down. Press the ends under ¼" again, and stitch down.

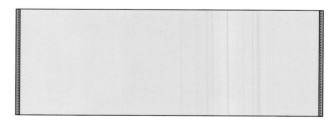

Press ends under ¼" and stitch in place; repeat.

**3** Press the strip in half lengthwise, wrong sides together. Place the raw edges of the folded strip against the top raw edge of the quilt, centering the strip. The ends of the strip should be ½" from the sides of the quilt. Hand baste the sleeve along the raw edges, starting at the sleeve's center and sewing to the ends in each direction. Sewing in this manner helps keep the sleeve centered.

**4** Bind the quilt as instructed in the next section. The top edge of the sleeve will be secured in the binding.

**5** After the binding strips are attached, smooth the sleeve down and pin into place. Hand sew the sides and bottom edge of the hanging sleeve to the quilt back, beginning at the center and working toward the ends. Be careful not to stitch through to the quilt front. Sew down only the bottom fabric layer of the sleeve when sewing the ends.

## - BINDING THE EDGES -

After your quilt has been quilted and a hanging sleeve basted into place if desired, it is time to sew on the binding. I use four separate binding strips, one for each side of the quilt.

**1** Measure the length of the quilt as you would for border strips. Cut two strips of fabric, 2¼" wide x the determined length, piecing if necessary. You can adjust the width of the strips to make a wider or narrower binding if you wish. These will be the binding strips for the sides.

**2** Press the strips in half lengthwise, wrong sides together. Pin a strip to each side of the front side of the quilt, aligning the binding raw edges with the quilt raw edge and the folded edge of the binding toward the center of the quilt. Sew the binding strips in place, using a ¼" seam allowance. I find that an even-feed foot keeps the layers lined up better and makes them less likely to slip around as I sew.

**3** Fold the binding up over the quilt edge, and then downward, covering all raw edges. Hand stitch it to the backing, being careful not to stitch through to the front.

**4** Measure the width of the quilt and add 2". Cut two strips, 2¼" wide x the determined length, for the top and bottom binding.

**5** Pin the top and bottom binding strips to the top and bottom edges of the front side of the quilt, leaving 1" extending beyond the quilt sides. Stitch into place. Trim the ends so that there is only ½" of excess fabric extending past the side binding.

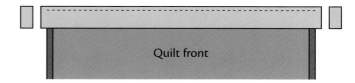

**6** Fold the binding up over the quilt's top edge, but not yet to the back side. Fold the excess binding on each end inward over the back side and over the side binding. Fold the remainder of the top binding strip downward to the quilt back, covering all raw edges; stitch into place.

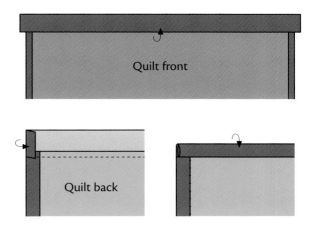

## ADDING A QUILT LABEL

It's always nice to personalize your quilt by adding a label to its backing. The label information can be as simple or detailed as you'd like. When making quilt labels, I include my name, the city and state where the quilt was made, the year of completion, and the fiber content of the fabric and batting. If the quilt was made for a particular person or occasion, I include that as well. In addition, I often put care instructions on the labels, especially if the quilt is a gift.

Labels can be hand stitched, machine stitched, or written and drawn by hand. It is helpful when writing or drawing your own label to iron a piece of freezer paper to the wrong side of the label fabric for stability. When using permanent-ink pens, always test them on a scrap of your label fabric before you begin writing.

# Making a Quilt Scrapbook

Now that your quilt is finished, consider making a quilt scrapbook. It's easy to do, especially if you gather the pertinent items for your scrapbook soon after your quilt's completion. If you've already made a number of quilts, don't worry, start your scrapbook with the quilt you've just completed and fill in with the ones you've already made as you can. The scrapbook makes a good reference book of the quilts you've already sewn, a good idea book for quilts you might want to sew, and a good recreation book for reminiscing.

To make a quilt scrapbook, I use a three-ring binder that was designed to hold photographs. This allows me to insert as many pages as I want, in addition to being able to move around the pages that I've already completed. Changing the order of the pages comes in handy, especially if you start your scrapbook after you've already finished a number of quilts and you want to present the quilts in a particular order, such as the chronological order of completion.

In my scrapbook, I use only full-size self-adhering photo pages that have no photo pockets. That way I can put whatever I want onto the page without being concerned about fitting items into a compartment of a predetermined size. If your scrapbook comes with pages that have photo pockets, ask the clerk if you can substitute full-size pages.

I generally use one scrapbook page per quilt. If each block of a quilt is substantially different and has a lot of intricate detail, I might use two. I like to include photographs of the completed front and back of the quilt; a front detail close-up; a label close-up that also shows the quilting stitches from the back; and, if the quilt was a gift, a photograph of the recipient. I also like to include a photograph of the back of the quilt top before it was layered and quilted, because this shows the piecing and pressing method used on the quilt top. I make the photographs no larger than 3" x 5", cutting them smaller if possible by trimming away any unnecessary portions of the photos.

In addition to the photographs, I also include a small scrap of all the major fabrics used in the quilt and a small descriptive notation about the quilt. The notation states pertinent information about the quilt, such as its name or pattern, date of completion, size, type of batting, whether it was tied or quilted, whether it was commissioned out for quilting, the name of the person who received the quilt if it was a gift, and any other relevant information. If the quilt was entered in a show or otherwise displayed, I would put that information here, too.

# Nine-Patch Charm

**Finished quilt size: 45½" x 45½" • Finished block size: 9" x 9"**

*I love charm quilts. I like looking at all the colors, designs, and textures of the blocks, each piece cut from a different fabric. I made my toddler grandson, Zachary, a 1930s charm quilt that fits comfortably into his car seat. Every time he rides in the car he examines and talks about the various figures and designs on his quilt. How fun!*

*"Nine-Patch Charm" is made with the 1930s fabrics that I enjoy so much. They are calming, subdued, warm, and comfortable, yet they are also intriguing with all their fine design detail. If you want to try a different flavor for your quilt, sew it with any fabric theme you desire, such as florals, plaids, solids, or batiks, or even make a one-color charm quilt.*

## - MATERIALS -

*All yardages are based on 42"-wide fabric.*

2 yards of white solid for blocks

Scraps measuring at least 3½" square of 65 different fabrics for Nine Patch blocks

½ yard of fabric for binding

3 yards of fabric for backing

50" x 50" piece of batting

4 skeins of red 6-strand embroidery floss

## - CUTTING -

*All measurements include ¼"-wide seam allowances.*

**From the white solid, cut:**

- 4 strips, 11½" x 42"; crosscut into 12 squares, 11½" x 11½"
- 5 strips, 3½" x 42"; crosscut into 52 squares, 3½" x 3½"

**From *each* of the 65 fabric scraps, cut:**

- 1 square, 3½" x 3½"

**From the binding fabric, cut:**

- 5 strips, 2¼" x 42"

## MAKING THE - REDWORK BLOCKS -

**1** Select 12 Sunbonnet Sue and Scottie patterns from pages 44–79 to use for the embroidered blocks. Refer to "Redwork" on page 15 to center and trace one design onto each of the white 11½" squares. Embroider each design with red floss.

**2** Press the completed blocks.

**3** Trim each block to 9½" x 9½", keeping the design centered.

## MAKING THE - NINE PATCH BLOCKS -

**1** Make two stacks of 3½" squares: one stack of 39 white squares and one stack of 39 scrap-fabric squares. Place the stacks next to your sewing machine.

**2** Chain piece the squares together in pairs so you have 39 units, each with one white square and one scrap-fabric square. Press the seam allowances toward the scrap-fabric squares.

 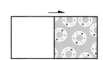

**3** Place 13 of the step 2 units in one stack and the remaining 13 white squares in another stack next to your sewing machine. Chain piece the white squares to the scrap-fabric end of the units to make row A. Press the seam allowances toward the scrap-fabric squares.

 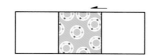

Row A.
Make 13.

**4** Place the remaining step 2 units in one stack and the remaining 26 scrap-fabric squares in another stack next to your sewing machine. Chain piece the scrap squares to the white-square end of the units to make row B. Press the seam allowances toward the scrap-fabric squares.

 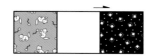

Row B.
Make 26.

**5** Place the row B units in one stack and the row A units in another stack next to your sewing machine. Sew one unit from each stack together, matching the seams. Press the seam allowances toward the row A units.

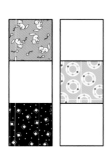 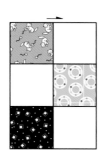

**6** Sew the remaining row B units to the step 5 units as shown to complete the Nine Patch blocks. Press the seam allowances toward the newly added row B units. Square up each block to 9½" x 9½", if needed.

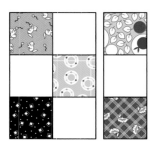 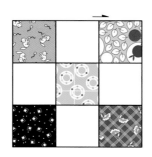

## ASSEMBLING
## - THE QUILT TOP -

Lay out the blocks in five horizontal rows as shown, alternating the blocks in each row and from row to row. Look at the overall appearance of the layout to see if you wish to reposition any of the blocks. Refer to "Quilts without Sashing" on page 22 to sew the blocks together to complete the quilt top.

Quilt assembly

## COMPLETING
## - YOUR QUILT -

Follow the information in "Putting It All Together" on page 22 to assemble the quilt layers, baste and quilt the layers together, add a hanging sleeve if desired, bind the quilt edges, and add a label.

# Checkerboard

Finished quilt size: 48" x 48" • Finished block size: 9" x 9"

*The vintage redwork quilts I've seen have all had simple basic settings to set off their wonderful embroidery. Some of the quilts had no sashings or borders at all. In these quilts the redwork blocks were lined up one after another across the quilt top, putting the total focus of the quilt on the redwork embroidery. Some of these beautiful quilts had a fine line of feather stitching along the connecting seam lines between the redwork blocks.*

*I've also seen vintage redwork quilts that had solid red sashing between the embroidered blocks. In some of these quilts the sashing was rather wide and in others it was narrow, but they were all basic and plain to set off the embroidered blocks.*

*Another frequently used setting I've seen consists of plain, solid-red blocks alternating with the embroidered blocks across the quilt top in checkerboard style. Some of these quilts had a solid red border around the outside edge and some did not. This checkerboard style is the setting that I've chosen to use here in "Checkerboard" and includes the use of a narrow border.*

## - MATERIALS -

*All yardages are based on 42"-wide fabric.*

2 yards of red solid for alternate blocks, border, and binding

1½ yards of white solid for Redwork blocks

3¼ yards of fabric for backing

52" x 52" piece of batting

4 skeins of red 6-strand embroidery floss

## - CUTTING -

*All measurements include ¼"-wide seam allowances.*

**From the white solid, cut:**

- 4 strips, 11½" x 42"; crosscut into 12 squares, 11½" x 11½"

**From the red solid, cut:**

- 4 strips, 9½" x 42"; crosscut into 13 squares, 9½" x 9½"
- 8 strips, 1¾" x 42"
- 5 strips, 2¼" x 42"

## MAKING THE - REDWORK BLOCKS -

**1** Select 12 Sunbonnet Sue and Scottie patterns from pages 44–79 to use for the embroidered blocks. Refer to "Redwork" on page 15 to center and trace one design onto each of the white 11½" squares. Embroider each design with red floss.

**2** Press the completed blocks.

**3** Trim each block to 9½" x 9½", keeping the design centered.

## ASSEMBLING - THE QUILT TOP -

**1** Lay out the Redwork blocks and red 9½" alternate blocks in five horizontal rows as shown in the quilt assembly diagram, alternating the blocks in each row and from row to row. Look at the overall appearance of the layout to see if you wish to reposition any of the blocks. Refer to "Quilts without Sashing" on page 22 to sew the blocks together to complete the quilt top.

**2** Sew two red 1¾" x 42" strips together end to end to make one long strip. Repeat to make a total of four strips. Press the seam allowances to one side.

3 Refer to "Adding Borders" on page 23 to measure the quilt length. Cut two of the pieced strips from step 2 to this measurement for the side borders, centering the seam allowances on the borders. You will cut off waste from each end of the borders.

4 Sew the borders to the sides of the quilt top, centering the seam line of each border strip with the center of the quilt sides.

5 Measure the quilt width, including the side borders, and repeat steps 3 and 4 with the remaining two pieced strips to add the top and bottom borders.

# COMPLETING
# - YOUR QUILT -

Follow the information in "Putting It All Together" on page 22 to assemble the quilt layers, baste and quilt the layers together, add a hanging sleeve if desired, bind the quilt edges, and add a label.

Quilt assembly

# All in Red

Finished quilt size: 42½" x 59" • Finished block size: 12" x 12"

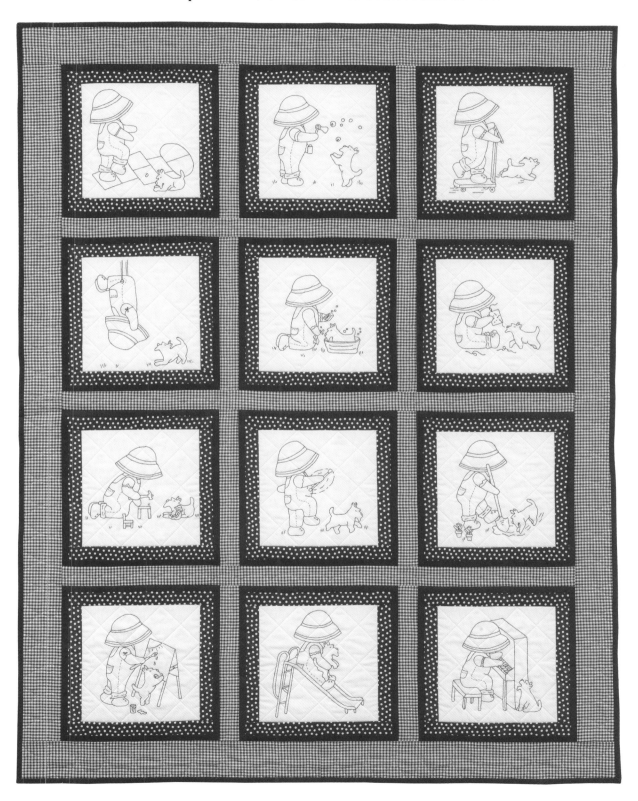

*Red, red, red! What a festive color! I asked my family what they "saw" when they thought of the color red. They said: roses, tulips, ladybugs on a vine, fresh cherries and apples, drippy cold Popsicles on a hot summer day . . . the Kool-Aid man, strawberry ice cream and sticky lollipops, Fourth of July fireworks, glowing embers in a fireplace . . . Valentine hearts, Santa's suit and candy canes, rosy cheeks on a winter's day, hot tomato soup . . . Grandma Zaruba, rubies, lipstick, blinky lights on people taking walks or riding bikes at night . . . barbershop poles, chili peppers, and bubbling marinara sauce. What does the color red make you think of?*

*Notice that this quilt embraces the playful Sues and Scotties with three values of the color red. Squint your eyes partway shut. Can you see the dark red—the solid fabric; the medium red—the polka-dot fabric; and the light red—the gingham-check fabric? "All in Red" brings a smile to all who see it.*

## - MATERIALS -

*All yardages are based on 42"-wide fabric.*

1½ yards of white solid for blocks

1⅓ yards of red gingham for sashing and border

1 yard of red solid for block outer borders and binding

⅔ yard of red-with-white polka-dot print for block inner borders

3 yards of fabric for backing

50" x 64" piece of batting

4 skeins of red 6-strand embroidery floss

## - CUTTING -

*All measurements include ¼"-wide seam allowances.*

**From the white solid, cut:**

- 4 strips, 11½" x 42"; crosscut into 12 squares, 11½" x 11½"

**From the red polka-dot print, cut:**

- 14 strips, 1½" x 42"; crosscut into:
  - 24 strips, 1½" x 11½"
  - 24 strips, 1½" x 9½"

**From the red solid, cut:**

- 16 strips, 1" x 42"; crosscut into:
  - 24 strips, 1" x 12½"
  - 24 strips, 1" x 11½"
- 6 strips, 2¼" x 42"

**From the red gingham, cut:**

- 6 strips, 2" x 42"; crosscut into:
  - 8 strips, 2" x 12½"
  - 3 strips, 2" x 39½"
- 8 strips, 3½" x 42"

## MAKING THE
## - REDWORK BLOCKS -

**1** Select 12 Sunbonnet Sue and Scottie patterns from pages 44–79 to use for the embroidered blocks. Refer to "Redwork" on page 15 to center and trace one design onto each of the white 11½" squares. Embroider each design with red floss.

**2** Press the completed squares.

**3** Trim each square to 9½" x 9½", keeping the design centered.

**4** Chain piece a polka-dot 1½" x 9½" strip to the right edge of each square. Repeat with the left edge of each square. Press the seam allowances toward the strips. The units should measure 11½" x 9½". Square up if necessary. Chain piece a polka-dot 1½" x 11½" strip to the top edge of each unit. Repeat with the bottom edge of each unit. Press the seam allowances toward the strips. The units should measure 11½" x 11½". Square up if necessary.

**5** Chain piece a red solid 1" x 11½" strip to the right edge of each unit from step 4. Repeat with the left edge of each unit. Press the seam allowances toward the red solid strips. The units should measure 12½" x 11½". Square up if necessary. Chain piece a red solid 1" x 12½" strip to the top edge of each unit. Repeat with the bottom edge of each unit to complete the

blocks. Press the seam allowances toward the red solid strips. The blocks should measure 12½" x 12½". Square up if necessary.

## ASSEMBLING
## - THE QUILT TOP -

**1** Lay out the blocks in four rows of three blocks each, leaving a little space between each block. Look at the overall appearance of the layout to see if you wish to reposition any of the blocks.

**2** When you are pleased with the block arrangement, place a red gingham 2" x 12½" strip between the blocks in each row. Place a red gingham 2" x 39½" sashing strip between each row.

**3** Refer to "Quilts with Sashing" on page 23 to sew the blocks and sashing strips together.

**4** Sew two red gingham 3½" x 42" strips together end to end to make one long strip. Repeat to make a total of four strips. Press the seam allowances to one side.

**5** Refer to "Adding Borders" on page 23 to measure the quilt length. Cut two of the pieced strips from step 4 to this measurement for the side borders, centering the seam allowances on the borders. You will cut off waste from each end of the borders.

**6** Sew the borders to the sides of the quilt top, centering the seam line of each border strip with the center of the quilt sides.

**7** Measure the quilt width, including the side borders, and repeat steps 5 and 6 with the remaining two pieced strips to add the top and bottom borders.

## COMPLETING
## - YOUR QUILT -

Follow the information in "Putting It All Together" on page 22 to assemble the quilt layers, baste and quilt the layers together, add a hanging sleeve if desired, bind the quilt edges, and add a label.

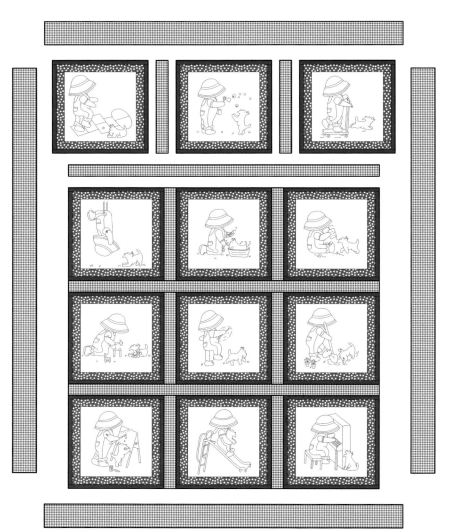

Quilt assembly

# Bordered in Blue

Finished quilt size: 44" x 44" • Finished block size: 11½" x 11½"

*Appliqué is such fun. When choosing and assembling the fabrics for Sue and Scottie, I almost felt like I was playing with paper dolls. You can dress your Sue in the same attire in each block of your quilt, as I did here, or you can choose a different fabric for Sue's outfit in each block. Scottie, too, can be whatever color you wish. Just imagine Sue and Scottie at play. The warm sun shines overhead and blue skies are all around.*

*I generally like to appliqué by hand using embroidery floss and a blanket stitch. It is very restful to me. In this quilt, however, I decided to do the blanket stitch by machine. The appliqué thread colors match the fabrics and are the same type used to piece the quilt. If you desire a more vintage look, you may want to consider using black thread to do all the machine appliqué. After appliquéing the design, come back and hand embroider the detail lines.*

## - MATERIALS -

*All yardages are based on 42"-wide fabric.*

1⅔ yards of white solid for blocks, sashing, and inner border

1 yard of blue fabric for block borders and outer border

1 fat quarter *each* of blue, gold, red, and brown fabrics for Sue's clothing

1 fat quarter of peach for Sue's arms and hands

1 fat quarter of black for Scottie appliqués

Scraps of assorted fabrics for remaining appliqué shapes

⅜ yard of fabric for binding

3 yards of fabric for backing

48" x 48" piece of batting

Paper-backed fusible transfer web

## - CUTTING -

*All measurements include ¼"-wide seam allowances.*

**From the white solid, cut:**

- 3 strips, 12½" x 42"; crosscut into 9 squares, 12½" x 12½"

- 8 strips, 2" x 42"; crosscut into:
  - 12 strips, 2" x 12"
  - 4 strips, 2" x 41"

**From the blue fabric, cut:**

- 12 strips, 1¼" x 42"; crosscut into:
  - 18 strips, 1¼" x 10½"
  - 18 strips, 1¼" x 12"

- 8 strips, 2" x 42"

**From the binding fabric, cut:**

- 5 strips, 2¼" x 42"

## – MAKING THE BLOCKS –

**1** Select nine Sunbonnet Sue and Scottie patterns from pages 44–79 to use for the appliquéd blocks. Refer to "Appliqué" on page 18 to create the appliqué shapes for each design, using the desired fabrics for each shape. Apply the shapes for each design to one white 12½" square so that the finished design is centered. Hand or machine stitch the pieces in place.

**2** Press the completed squares.

**3** Trim each square to 10½" x 10½", keeping the design centered.

**4** Chain piece a blue 1¼" x 10½" strip to the right edge of each square. Repeat with the left edge of each square. Press the seam allowances toward the strips. The units should measure 12" x 10½". Square up if necessary. Chain piece a blue 1¼" x 12" strip to the top edge of each unit. Repeat with the bottom edge of each unit to complete the blocks. Press the seam allowances toward the strips. The blocks should measure 12" x 12". Square up if necessary.

## ASSEMBLING – THE QUILT TOP –

**1** Lay out the blocks in three rows of three blocks each, leaving a little space between each block. Look at the overall appearance of the layout to see if you wish to reposition any of the blocks.

**2** When you are pleased with the block arrangement, place a white 2" x 12" sashing strip between the blocks in each row and at the beginning and end of each row. Place a white 2" x 41" sashing strip between each row, above the first row, and below the last row.

**3** Refer to "Quilts with Sashing" on page 23 to sew the blocks and sashing strips together.

**4** Sew two blue 2" x 42" strips together end to end to make one long strip. Repeat to make a total of four strips for the outer borders. Press the seam allowances to one side.

**5** Refer to "Adding Borders" on page 23 to measure the quilt length. Cut two of the pieced strips from step 4 to this measurement for the side borders, centering the seam allowances on the borders. You will cut off waste from each end of the borders.

**6** Sew the borders to the sides of the quilt top, centering the seam line of each border strip with the center of the quilt sides.

**7** Measure the quilt width, including the side borders, and repeat steps 5 and 6 with the remaining two pieced strips to add the top and bottom borders.

Quilt assembly

## COMPLETING – YOUR QUILT –

Follow the information in "Putting It All Together" on page 22 to assemble the quilt layers, baste and quilt the layers together, add a hanging sleeve, bind the quilt edges, and add a label.

# Bordered in Green

Finished quilt size: 33½" x 33½" • Finished block size: 10" x 10"

*When I was young, my mother and I traveled all over the western United States in our little Volkswagen Beetle. At night, we stopped at national parks and camped among the tall trees and beautiful scenery. While we unpacked to set up our campsite, nearby campers stood around and stared as we pulled out our camping supplies, including a four-person tent, from the various nooks and crannies of our small car. Everyone was friendly and we always had a good time. I've always enjoyed the outdoors and have planted as many trees and flowers in my Arizona desert backyard as it can support.*

*This quilt was designed using two different genres of fabric—folk-style fabrics for the appliqué blocks and a beautiful forest-green batik for the borders. Doesn't this fun combination give you the feeling of being in the great outdoors?*

## - MATERIALS -

*All yardages are based on 42"-wide fabric.*

⅞ yard of light beige solid for blocks

⅞ yard of green leaf print for sashing cornerstones, outer border, and binding

⅜ yard of light green print for sashing

¼ yard of beige print for inner border

Scraps of assorted fabrics for appliqués

1¼ yards of fabric for backing

40" x 40" piece of batting

## - CUTTING -

*All measurements include ¼"-wide seam allowances.*

**From the light beige solid, cut:**

- 2 strips, 12½" x 42"; crosscut into 4 squares, 12½" x 12½"

**From the light green print, cut:**

- 4 strips, 2½" x 42"; crosscut into 12 rectangles, 2½" x 10½"

**From the green leaf print, cut:**

- 4 strips, 2½" x 42"; crosscut 1 strip into 9 squares, 2½" x 2½"
- 4 strips, 3½" x 42"
- 4 strips, 2¼" x 42"

**From the beige print, cut:**

- 4 strips, 1" x 42"

## - MAKING THE BLOCKS -

**1** Select four Sunbonnet Sue and Scottie patterns from pages 44–79 to use for the appliquéd blocks. Refer to "Appliqué" on page 18 to create the appliqué shapes for each design, using the desired fabrics for each shape. Apply the shapes for each design to one light beige 12½" square so that the finished design is centered. Hand or machine stitch the pieces in place. After appliquéing the design, hand embroider the detail lines.

**2** Press the completed squares.

**3** Trim each square to 10½" x 10½", keeping the design centered.

## ASSEMBLING
## - THE QUILT TOP -

**1** Lay out the blocks in two rows of two blocks each, leaving a little space between each block. Look at the overall appearance of the layout to see if you wish to reposition any of the blocks.

**2** When you are pleased with the block arrangement, place a light green 2½" x 10½" sashing rectangle between the blocks in each row and at the beginning and end of each row. Place another light green rectangle at the top of each block and at the bottom of each block in the second row. Fill in the spaces between the sashing rectangles with a leaf print 2½" x 2½" sashing cornerstone. Refer to the quilt assembly diagram if necessary.

**3** Refer to "Quilts with Sashing" on page 23 to sew the blocks and sashing rectangles in each block row together, and then sew the sashing rectangles and sashing cornerstones in each sashing row together. Sew the sashing rows and block rows together.

**4** Refer to "Adding Borders" on page 23 to measure the quilt length. Cut two of the beige print 1" x 42" strips to this measurement for the inner side borders.

**5** Sew the borders to the sides of the quilt top.

**6** Measure the quilt width, including the inner side borders, and cut the remaining two beige print strips to this measurement for the inner top and bottom borders. Sew the borders to the top and bottom of the quilt top.

**7** Repeat step 4 with the leaf print 3½" x 42" strips to add the outer borders to the quilt top.

Quilt assembly

## COMPLETING
## - YOUR QUILT -

Follow the information in "Putting It All Together" on page 22 to assemble the quilt layers, baste and quilt the layers together, add a hanging sleeve if desired, bind the quilt edges, and add a label.

# *The Block Patterns*

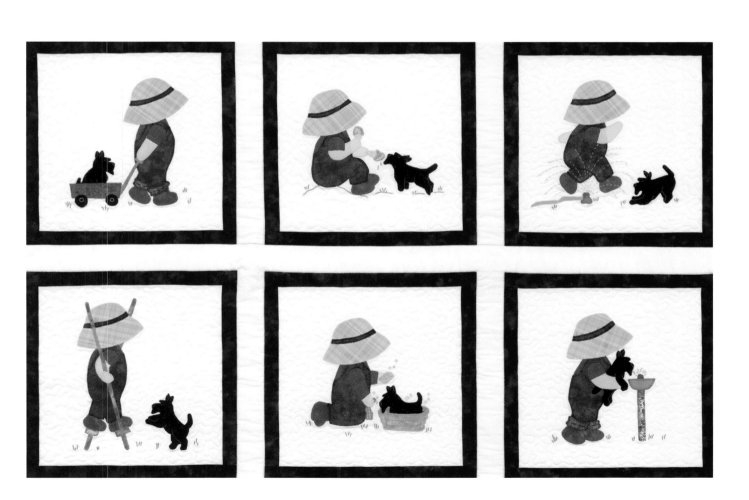

# - AT A TEA PARTY -

**Stitch key**

——— Stem stitch

– – – Running stitch

✕✕ Cross-stitch

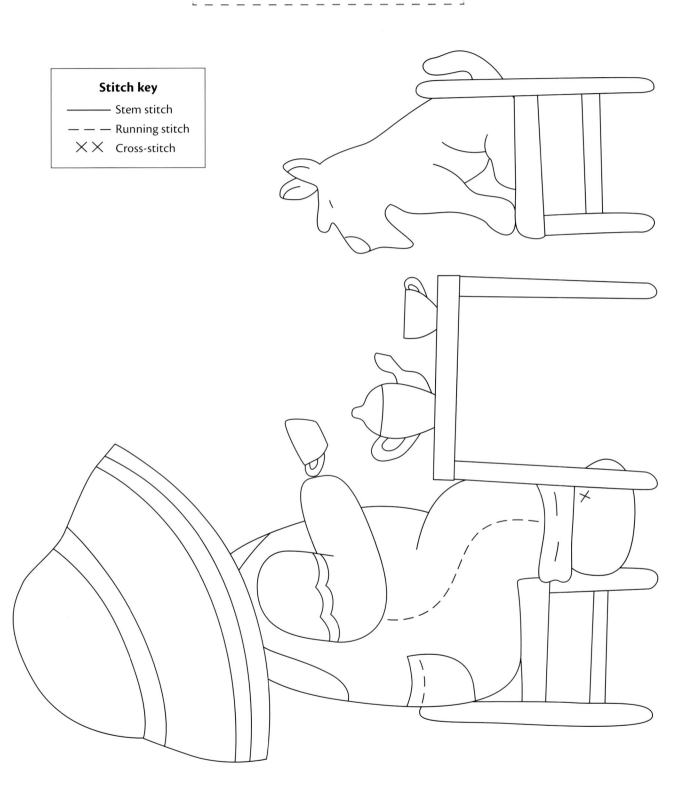

# - BARBECUING -

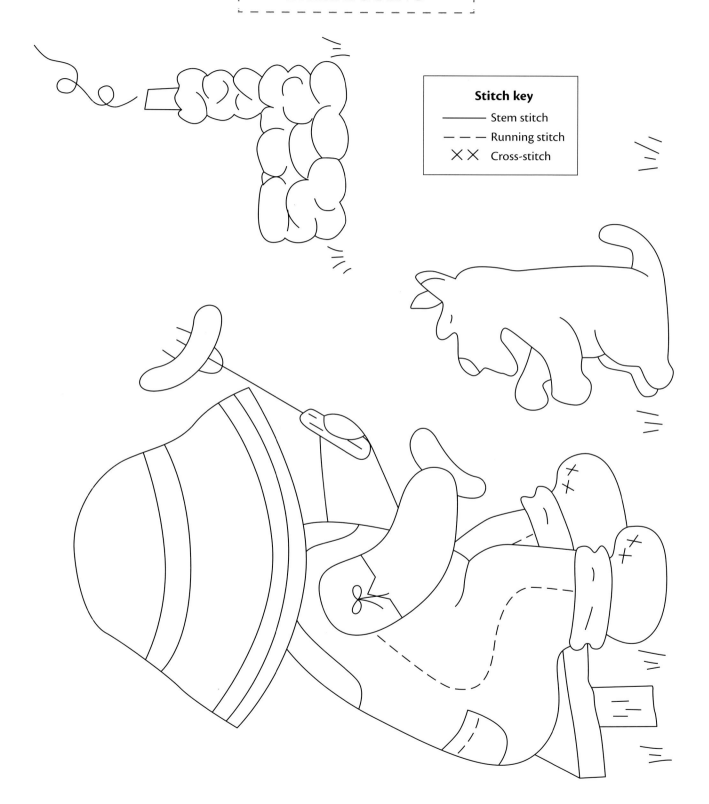

**Stitch key**

——— Stem stitch

- - - Running stitch

✕ ✕ Cross-stitch

# - BATHING SCOTTIE -

**Stitch key**

—— Stem stitch

- - - Running stitch

✕ ✕ Cross-stitch

# - BLOWING BUBBLES -

**Stitch key**
— Stem stitch
- - - Running stitch
✕✕ Cross-stitch

# - BUILDING DOLL FURNITURE -

**Stitch key**

—— Stem stitch

- - - Running stitch

XX Cross-stitch

# - CAMPING -

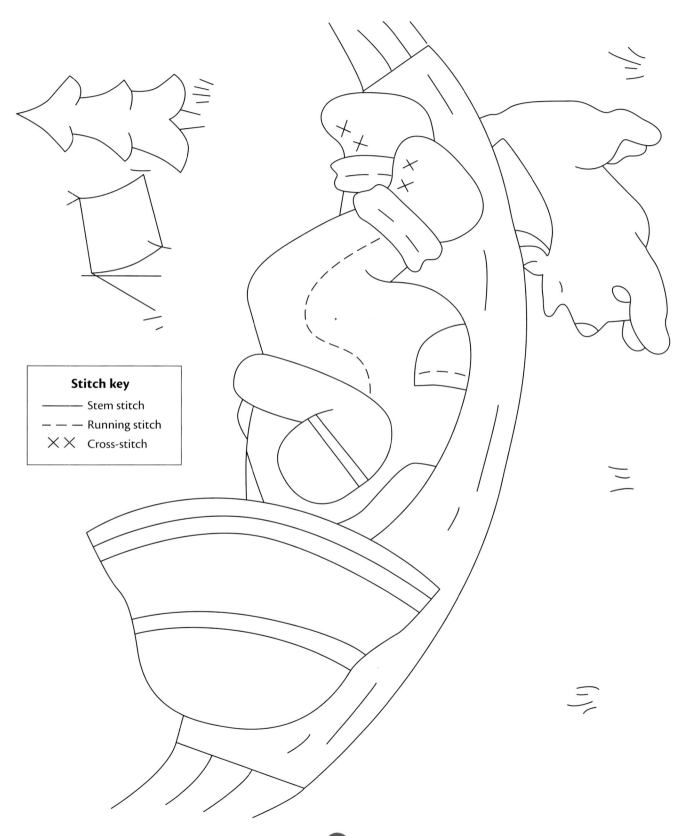

**Stitch key**

——— Stem stitch

– – – Running stitch

✕ ✕ Cross-stitch

## - CLIMBING A TREE -

**Stitch key**
——— Stem stitch
- - - Running stitch
✕✕ Cross-stitch

# - COLORING -

**Stitch key**

—————— Stem stitch

– – – – Running stitch

✕ ✕ Cross-stitch

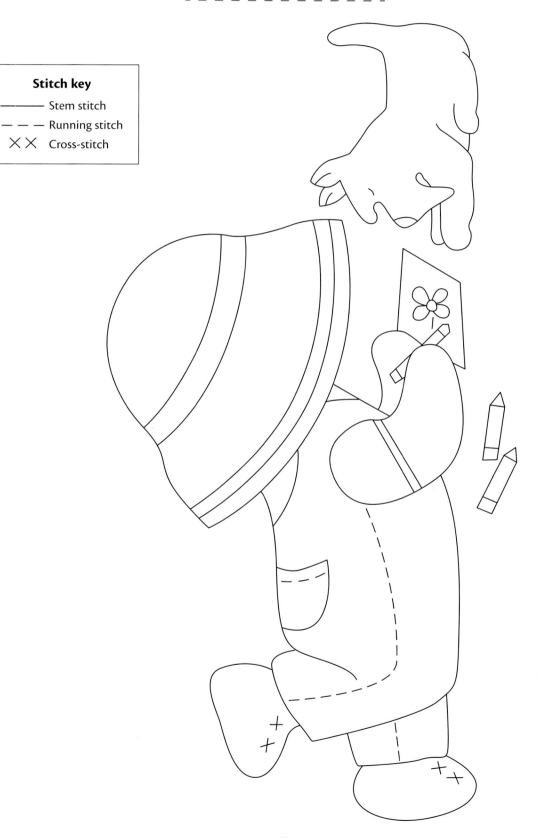

## - EATING ICE CREAM -

**Stitch key**

—————— Stem stitch

— — — — Running stitch

✕✕ Cross-stitch

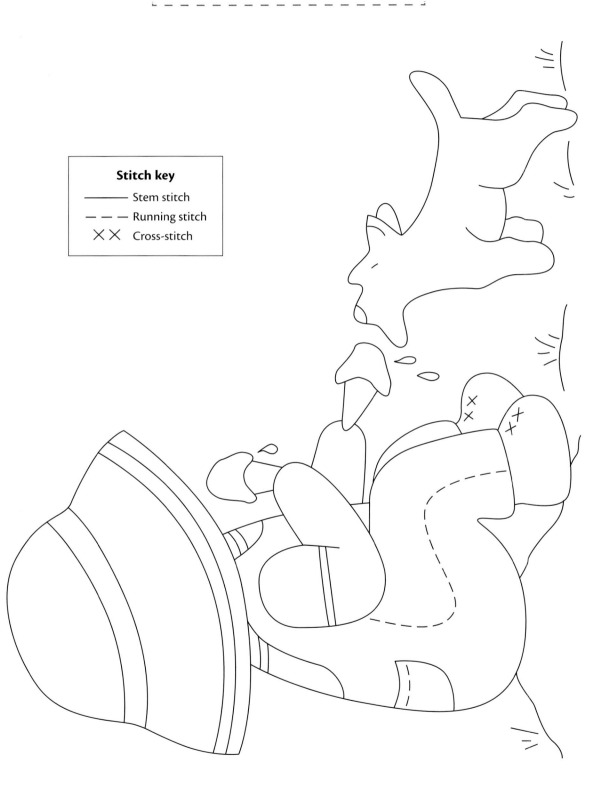

# - FLYING A KITE -

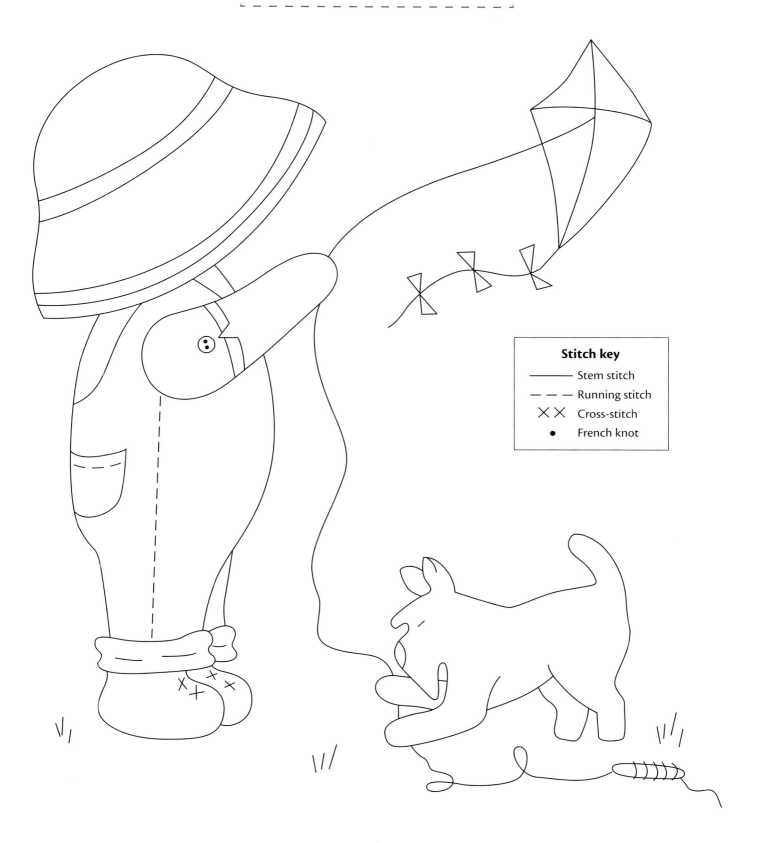

**Stitch key**
— Stem stitch
- - - Running stitch
✕✕ Cross-stitch
● French knot

# - GETTING A DRINK -

**Stitch key**
⎯⎯ Stem stitch
⎯ ⎯ Running stitch
✕✕ Cross-stitch

# - HIKING -

**Stitch key**

— Stem stitch

- - - Running stitch

✕✕ Cross-stitch

● French knot

# - IN A SPRINKLER -

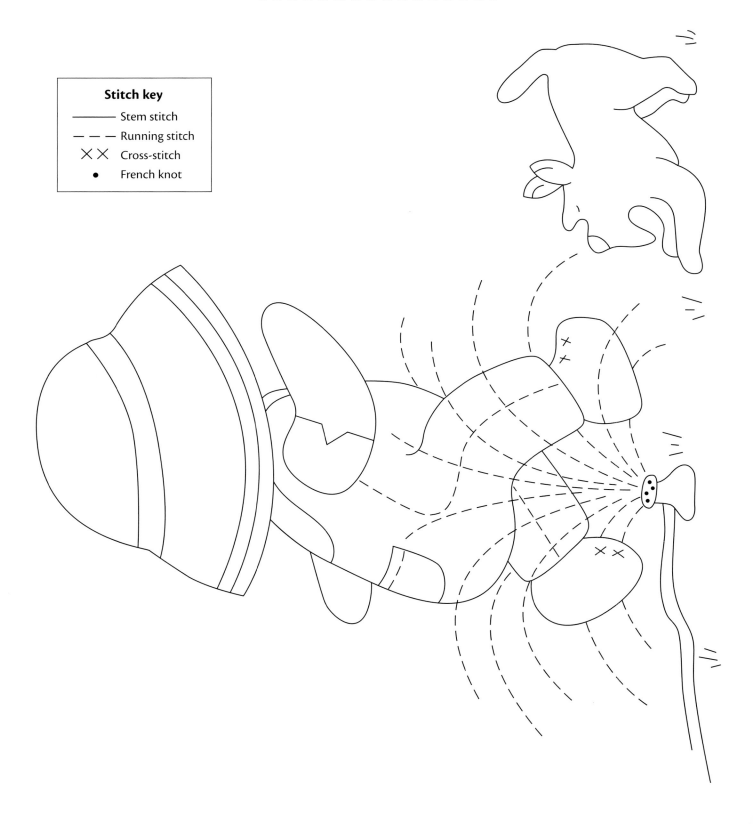

**Stitch key**

——— Stem stitch

— — — Running stitch

× × Cross-stitch

● French knot

# - IN THE SAND -

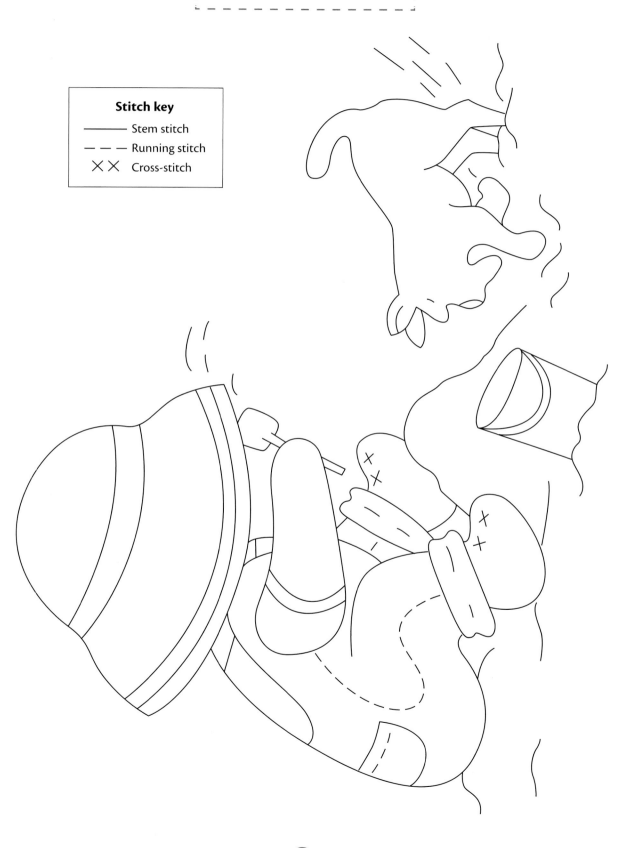

**Stitch key**

— Stem stitch

- - - Running stitch

✕ ✕ Cross-stitch

## - JUMPING ROPE -

**Stitch key**

—— Stem stitch

– – – Running stitch

✕✕ Cross-stitch

# - ON A HOBBY HORSE -

**Stitch key**

——— Stem stitch

– – – Running stitch

✕✕ Cross-stitch

• French knot

# - ON A SLIDE -

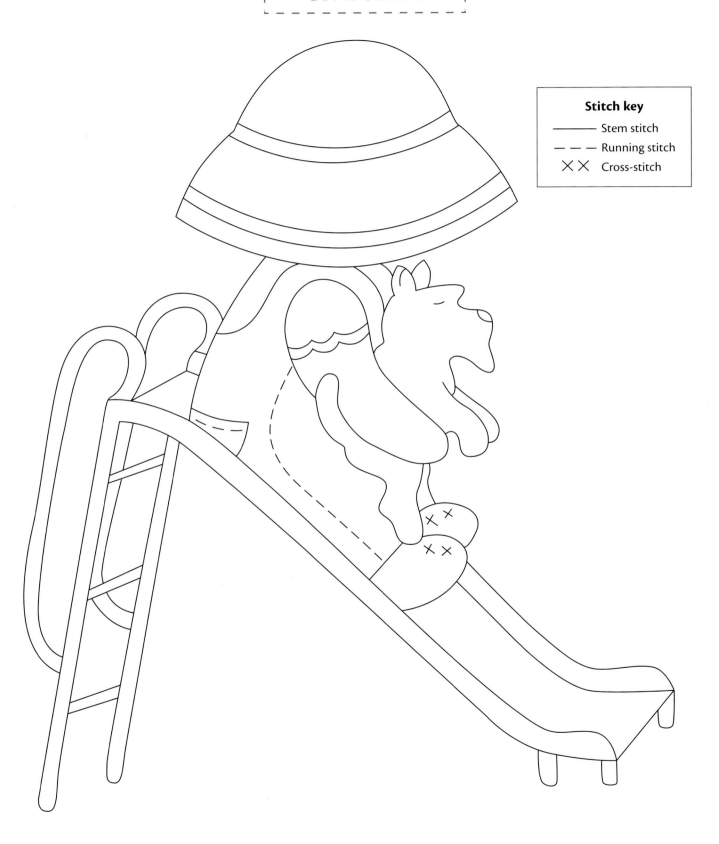

**Stitch key**

—————— Stem stitch

– – – – – Running stitch

✕ ✕ Cross-stitch

# - ON A TRAPEZE -

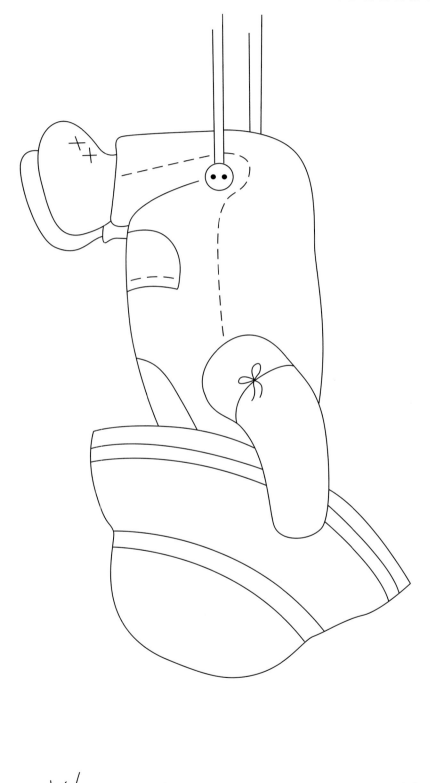

**Stitch key**

| | |
|---|---|
| —— | Stem stitch |
| - - - | Running stitch |
| ✕ ✕ | Cross-stitch |
| • | French knot |

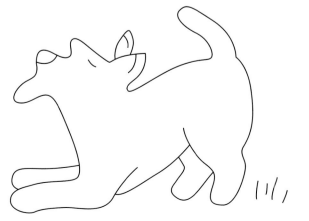

# - ON STILTS -

**Stitch key**
- Stem stitch
- - - - Running stitch
- ✕✕ Cross-stitch

# - PAINTING -

**Stitch key**
— Stem stitch
- - - Running stitch
✕ ✕ Cross-stitch

# - PLANTING FLOWERS -

**Stitch key**

—— Stem stitch

- - - Running stitch

✕ ✕ Cross-stitch

# - PLAYING BALL -

**Stitch key**

—————— Stem stitch

– – – – Running stitch

✕ ✕  Cross-stitch

•  French knot

# - PLAYING HOPSCOTCH -

**Stitch key**

——— Stem stitch

— — — Running stitch

✕ ✕ Cross-stitch

# - PLAYING JACKS -

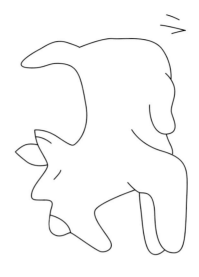

**Stitch key**

——— Stem stitch

— — — Running stitch

✕ ✕  Cross-stitch

⊕  Satin stitch

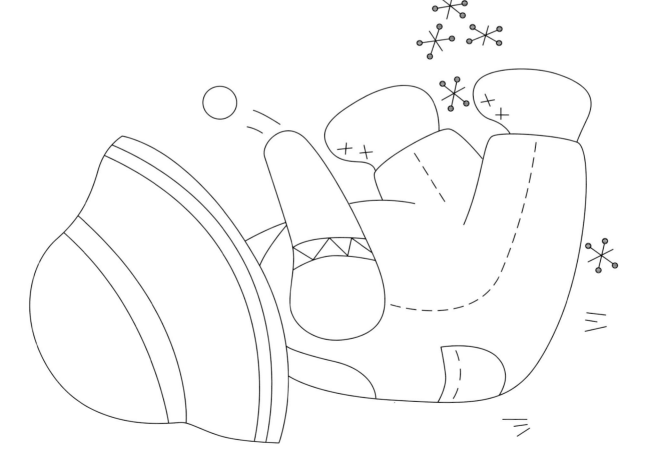

# - PLAYING PADDLEBALL -

**Stitch key**
—— Stem stitch
– – – Running stitch
✕✕ Cross-stitch

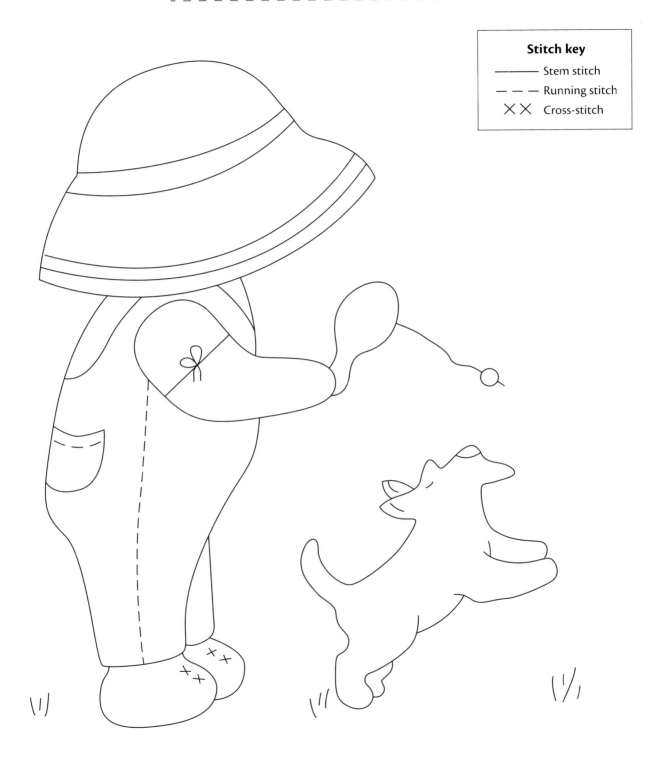

# - PLAYING PIANO -

**Stitch key**

—————— Stem stitch

— — — Running stitch

✕ ✕ Cross-stitch

● French knot

# - PLAYING WITH A HULA HOOP -

**Stitch key**

—————— Stem stitch

- - - - - Running stitch

✕ ✕ Cross-stitch

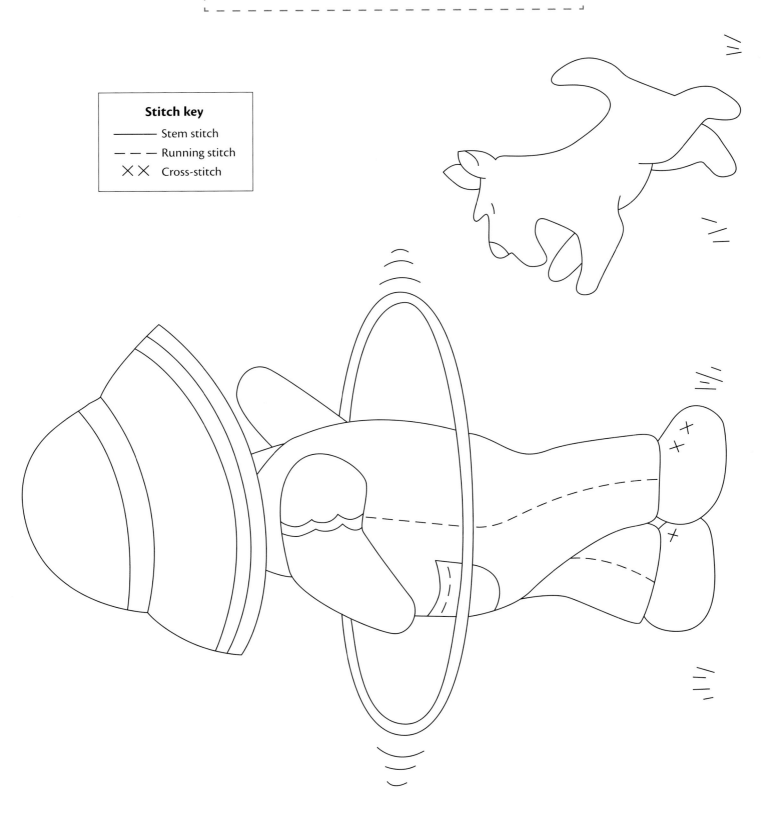

# - PLAYING WITH BLOCKS -

**Stitch key**

——— Stem stitch

– – – Running stitch

✕✕ Cross-stitch

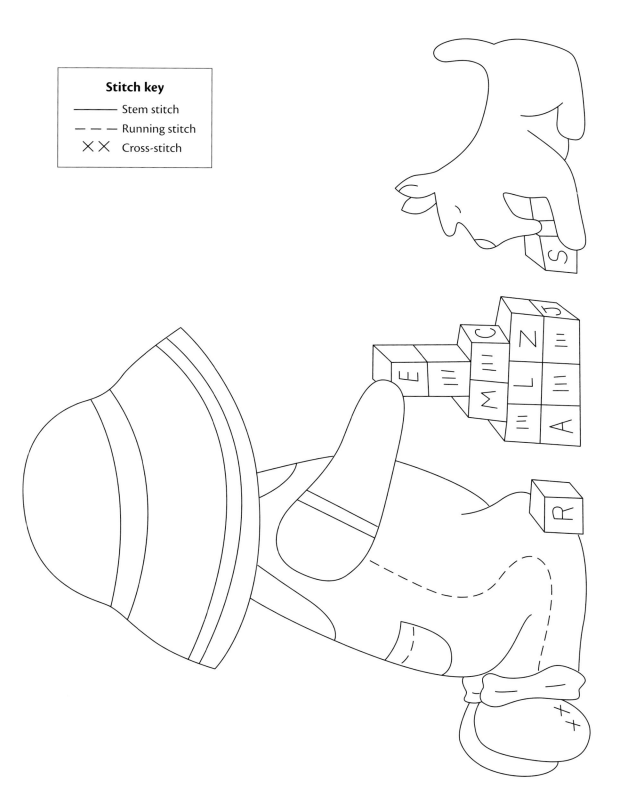

# - PULLING A WAGON -

**Stitch key**

——— Stem stitch

– – – Running stitch

XX Cross-stitch

# - READING -

**Stitch key**

— Stem stitch

– – – Running stitch

✕✕ Cross-stitch

# - RIDING A SCOOTER -

**Stitch key**

─────── Stem stitch

─ ─ ─ ─ Running stitch

✕ ✕ Cross-stitch

● French knot

# – ROLLER-SKATING –

**Stitch key**

——— Stem stitch

– – – Running stitch

✕ ✕ Cross-stitch

# - SAILING A TOY BOAT -

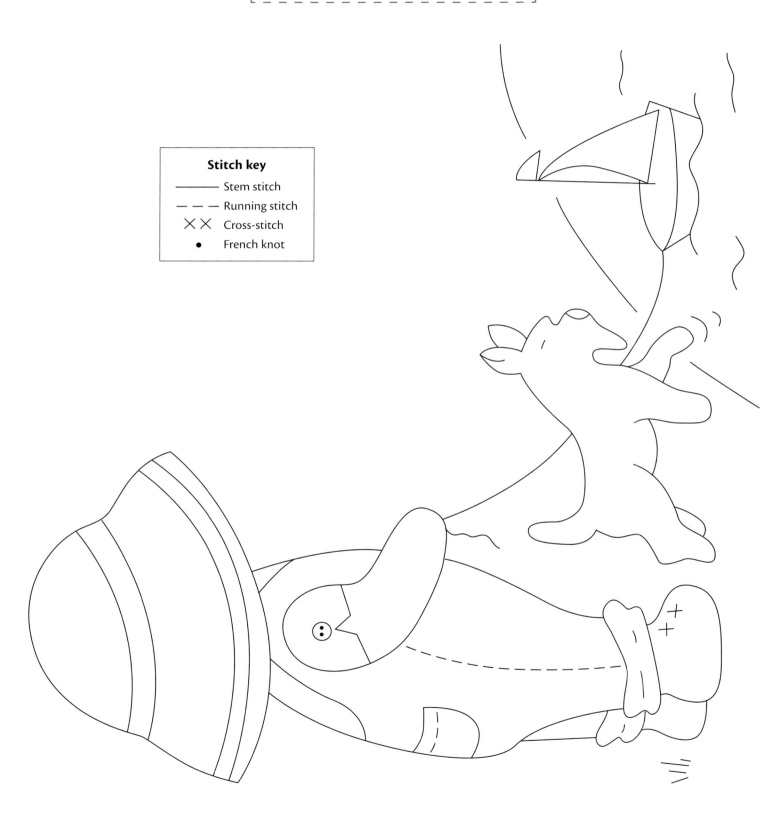

**Stitch key**

——— Stem stitch

— — — Running stitch

✕ ✕ Cross-stitch

● French knot

# - SEWING -

**Stitch key**
- Stem stitch
- - - Running stitch
- ✗ ✗ Cross-stitch
- ● French knot

# - SWINGING -

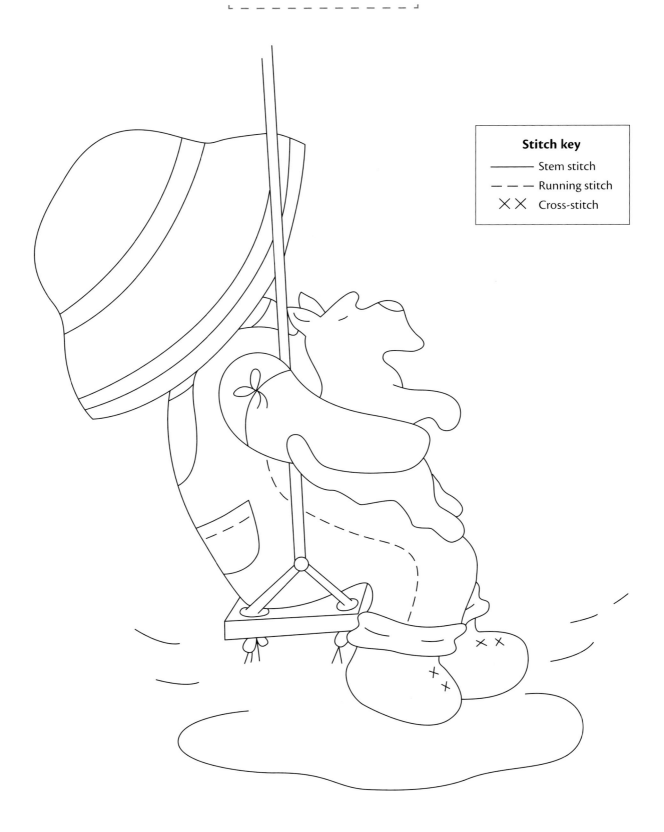

**Stitch key**

—————— Stem stitch

— — — Running stitch

✕ ✕ Cross-stitch

# - TWIRLING A BATON -

**Stitch key**

——— Stem stitch

- - - Running stitch

✕✕ Cross-stitch

# *About the Author*

Suzanne Zaruba Cirillo lives in Tempe, Arizona, with her husband, son, and two Cavalier King Charles spaniels, Lady and Maggie. She has been making beautiful quilts for her family and friends since the early 1970s. Her interest in quilting was stimulated in her early childhood when she and her sister each received a lavender Nine Patch scrappy quilt from their maternal aunt. This was the first quilt that she remembers seeing, and she treasured it for many years.

Suzanne was introduced to sewing as a child in National City, California, where her family lived while her father was serving in the U.S. Navy. Her mother took Suzanne and her sister to local parks-and-recreation programs where they participated in needlework classes, among other things. After graduating from San Diego State College, Suzanne married her husband, Richard, and had three children: Christine, Michael, and Elizabeth. She enjoyed sewing her family's clothing. Her first quilts were for her children, and the appliqué quilt that she made for her youngest daughter's third birthday is still loved and in daily use today after three decades.